WE *the new* ME

TAMARE HOUSE

We The New Me

7 LEVELS OF SELF AWARENESS FOR BUILDING EFFECTIVE TEAMS

Written by Debbii McKoy
Published with the services of TamaRe House Publishers Ltd, UK, 2009
www.tamarehouse.com – info@tamarehouse.com - +44 207 978 8321

Cover by Fiona Dempsey
Printed by Lightning Source, UK, 2009

ISBN: 978-1-906169-13-8

WE *the new* ME

7 LEVELS OF SELF AWARENESS FOR BUILDING EFFECTIVE TEAMS

DEBBII MCKOY

$\mathcal{D}$edication

This book is for my Nan, Gladys "Miss May" McKoy

and my late Grandad, Edgar McKoy.

Acknowledgements

This book is the result of my thirty four years of holding a well-defined self-image and taking the options open to me at each stage in my life. The journey of life takes us in many directions. At times the roads we travel are not sign-posted, and the only indication we are going in the right direct are the guides we meet along the way. Of all my many teachers, I especially want to thank Joe Adams for sharing his fifty years of sales knowledge and experience so generously with me. He has profoundly simplified what I have come to understand as an art, and has taken the time to expand my awareness of my own ability.

I would also like to thank Raymond Walley for all his witty stories, which have helped me grasp the dominating factors of different personality types. Both he and Joe have shown so much belief in me, making it easier for me to live up to their expectations.

I'd also like to extend my warmest gratitude to Camille Bradstreet, without whom this book would not have been possible. As you said Camille, we've reached the pinnacle. The real fun comes when we allow the momentum to drive the ride, and this is where the real fun is! Here comes the thrill of all the effort.

To my sons, Joel, Vaughny, and Mikey, I thank you with all my heart for your adoring love and for allowing me to share my many adventures with you.

To my family, thank you for your love and support, and for always believing in me.

Testimonials

"In *We The New Me* Debbii McKoy breaks down the individual and collective mindset needed to build an effective team in a coherent and digestible manner. Debbii then proceeds to build the mindset back up again thought by thought, empowering you to take responsibility and control of your circumstances. The strategies for change in the book are embedded in sound and time honoured principles. Debbii is both empathic and pragmatic in her writing which guided me to an even great level of self-awareness of myself and my interaction with others. This book truly provides an understanding of why and how an individual's dreams and aspirations can only be met through the collective effort of a team."

Ken Barnes,
Author of The Seven Principles of RESPECTisms

"I've always tried to explain to the faint-hearted, the timorous and the plain scared that what you need to succeed is confidence. Style helps, and if style and confidence are added to a taste for hard work, there really is no stopping you. There's no such thing as an ambitious, stylish and energetic person who fails. Debbii McKoy is proof".

Stephen Bayley,
British Design Critic, Cultural Commentator and Author.

"Debbii McKoy's powerhouse self-development book increases your level of awareness to maximize your potential in working with others. The skills you can quickly develop using the sage guidance of We The New Me, puts others at ease in your presence, creating greater trust in your integrity. You'll become a stronger team member who walks humbly yet confidently, strives to continually develop talents and abilities, and compliments the talents of others. Clients will know you as a person with whom they want to do business. You will benefit from the treasures in this book for years to come."

Paul R. Scheele,
author of PhotoReading and Natural Brilliance, co-founder of Learning Strategies Corporation, and international consultant on human development.

Testimonials

"In this fantastic book Debbii McKoy explains that the ability to effectively communicate with your colleagues, associates, employees, and business partners is of great importance in creating a dynamic team. As your level of awareness increases and you begin to maximize your potential, you can quickly and effortlessly allow others to feel at ease in your presence, trust in your integrity, and want to do business with you. A strong team member is one who walks humbly yet confidently, and who strives to continually develop their talents and abilities to the degree that they are successful in whatever they do whilst complimenting the talents of others."

Gerry Robert,
Bestselling author of The Millionaire Mindset

"To understand what is going on in our lives, and indeed to change it, we must begin to understand the role that our thoughts play. It is said that we only use ten percent of our mind's true potential. What happened to all the rest? Reading this book cemented the things that I already know, and also revealed to me much that I didn't. When I first met Debbii McKoy, her passion for her subject was obvious. After we did a short 'Psychometric Profile', I was truly amazed at how accurate and revealing it was about my personality. You too will find out, in these pages that follow, that the causes of the things that are happening to you in your life lie within you. You have the power."

Kevin Minter-Brown,
Teacher of John Kehoe's Mind Power, UK

Table of Contents

Chapter 1 –   Who Do YOU Think You ARE?   15

Chapter 2 –   You Weren't Born Rich? So What!   39

Chapter 3 –   It's YOUR Power! Taking it Back and Keeping it   57

Chapter 4 –   Coincidence? I Think Not!   73

Chapter 5 –   Moving Forward -

               Now That You Understand Where You've Been   87

Chapter 6 –   Unintended Outcomes –

               Responding With Focus Rather Than

               Reacting With Emotions   103

Chapter 7 –   Seven Levels of Awareness for Success   115

Chapter 8 –   Presenting Yourself –

               You Never Get a Second Chance to Make a

               First Impression   135

Chapter 9 –   When Your Song Hits the Charts!   151

Chapter 10 –   The Good Life Awaits   161

Introduction

The good life awaits you. Are you ready? Do you even know what you want? Making goals is not a difficult task for most people, but achieving those goals, or dreams, can sometimes seem to be "the impossible dream." Throughout this book, *We the New Me* I am proposing a way to understand how your mind works in order to help you figure out which positions on a "team" suit you best. Once we find a niche, then we can press forward toward our dreams as a solid team member. I do this with a process called Psychometric Analysis.

But developing the strong team player is not the only aim for this book. I would also like to help improve your thinking, and find a way to encourage the artist in you. Everyone has some sort of artistic abilities; the key is to find out what they are, be they in fine arts or "the art of the deal," to borrow a phrase from Donald Trump. Finding your spot on the team, figuring out your artistic path, and then learning to think like a successful businessperson will lead you to being able to fulfill lifelong desires of achieving wealth and fame, if you so desire, and happiness, most of all.

I tell my story as a successful song lyricist with two hits, one which hit the top five of the British National Charts. Understanding the nature and volatility of the music industry, however, I directed my earnings into other entrepreneurial ventures which have led me to where I am now. As a public speaker and Life Coach with LifeSuccess Consultants, I now have the honour of sharing my knowledge, experience and hope for the brightest future with you in this book and via the other forms of communication I use.

As with any journey in life, the road to success has smooth roads, and potholes and pitfalls. How to be a well-balanced individual who understands his or her personality, strengths, weaknesses, artistic talents, and most of all, desires and intended outcomes, will all be addressed.

I've used examples of the famous, the infamous, and the not-so-famous to get my point across to people of all ages, sexes, races and backgrounds. Success is available to you no matter what your background is, what education you have or don't have, or skill levels you think you possess or lack. You can be a winner on the team. Understanding team dynamics will be revealed in an easy-to-follow explanation, and I aim to show you that in order to be truly successful, you must surround yourself with team players who share your vision. I will encourage you to examine your surroundings and decide if your circle of influence supports you in becoming who you are, or, as it is for many, if it tends to drain you.

But at the end of it all, I share that you are not alone. I am here to help you along your path of success. I'll share my knowledge and show you that you are in good company. It doesn't have to be lonely at the top. Attitudes toward real success are all around you. Seek the positive. You'll then be surrounded by positive people and influences.

I'm glad you've decided to join me on this journey.

Debbii McKoy

Chapter One

Who do You Think You Are?

Chapter One

Who do You Think You Are?

From Merriam Webster's Online Dictionary

Main Entry: *art·ist*

Pronunciation: *'är-tist*

Function: **noun**

1: one skilled or versed in learned arts; **2a:** one who professes and practices an imaginative art; b: a person skilled in one of the fine arts; **3:** a skilled performer; especially, **4:** one who is adept at something

Everyone is an artist. How do you feel about that statement? Everyone is an artist. I do mean everyone. Isn't it brilliant that throughout history, the idea of an artist has evolved? It is easy to spot celebrity artists, sports figures such as David Beckham, so accomplished at their game they seem super-human, or the fine art talent displayed in museums (too numerous to even mention) or alongside city streets, but do you know you are an artist? You may have approached this book in search of finding your path in life to greater financial fortune, but that fortune lies within yourself. Some people are artistic with oil paints, watercolours or sculpting clay; others with a guitar or piano, or some may be an adept artist investing in the stock market. Yet rarely do successful individuals respond to the question, "how did you make your fortune?" by stating that he or she plunged headfirst into a field that was totally distasteful or uninspiring. They often respond with the phrase, "I always loved...."

So, what do you love to do? If you cannot answer that question, don't fret. This book is intended to help you sort out your passions and strengths in combination with what you are good at, and then help you make a plan to get you to realise your purpose, vision and goals – including large numbers reflected in your bank account! I want to help you to find your artistic strength by initially figuring out how your mind works, and how that knowledge of your personality and its positive attributes can bring you financial and personal success. True success encompasses all areas of life.

ABOUT ME

I am an artist. My name is Debbii McKoy. I am a songwriter, musician, businesswoman, and loving mother of three incredible boys. I am a devoted daughter, an adoring granddaughter, and an active participant in creating the life I desire. I am a LifeSuccess Consultant and public speaker, and my experience as a certified Psychometric Analyst, and employing the concepts of this fascinating technique, is a great asset to helping others find the artist within.

Though I knew early on in life that I loved composing poetry and song lyrics and that my family was a priority in my life, I didn't know where this passion would take me or how it would bring abundance into my life. In fact, I was raised in a crowded home in an inner-city London neighbourhood. My mother was young and unwed, and we lived in my grandparents' cramped top floor flat; I didn't even meet my father until I was five. I was hardly privileged, as most people will define it. I knew that I was loved and was encouraged to achieve by my mother and grandparents. They always told me I was wonderful and that I could achieve anything and everything.

Yet my upbringing was unstructured. It was not uncommon at the time for the children to be "sent out to play." There was an expectation that we were safe. Children of my neighbourhood were exposed to many ideas and practices such as crime and drugs, but, unlike the majority of youngsters who grew up in my neighbourhood, I managed to come through exposure to these dream-crushing behaviours unscathed. I thank God for that, but I do think that my lucky escape from totally allowing myself to be gobbled up by these habits and choices came about because I was encouraged to be great. That was how I was programmed early on.

I also knew that I wanted to contribute to popular music and communicate my passion for it to the world. If I could succeed at that, then how else could I affect the world? One of my songs hit number four on the British charts. In retrospect, all I did was set my intention to have a hit song, act on this desire by a constant habit of creating poetry and song lyrics, and then the desire manifested with very little effort on my part when a friend recorded my song. I'd shared my art with my friends all along, and my circle of influence knew that I made the effort to copyright my material.

They always told me I was wonderful and that I could achieve anything and everything.

FINDING OUT
ABOUT YOU

The opening of this chapter is asking about you. Who do YOU think you ARE? What is your self-image? How were you programmed early on in your life? By programmed (the nature versus nurture debate), I mean conscious or unconscious statements by those around you – parents, grandparents, extended family, neighbours, teachers, or schoolmates? Were comments to you, and about you, positive or negative? Were you told you were beautiful, ugly, intelligent or an idiot; were your skills and talents complimented or discouraged?

Does this matter in how one sees oneself? Indeed it does. How we are programmed as a child has such a profound effect on how we see ourselves as adults. And I do not mean to imply that your parents, teachers or any others were bad people by negatively reinforcing any ideas which may have impacted you. As a parent, I know that it absolutely pains me to see one of my boys experience disappointment or "failure." I put that in quotes, because I don't see many things as failures. Rather, I see these disappointments as life lessons or redirections. It can help us define what we want by realizing what we definitely do not want. Our experiences directly create our thoughts, which often create who we think we are!

YOUR THOUGHTS

The thoughts we hold in our mind are shown in the results we achieve through our actions. We have private conversations with ourselves that we carry on "inside our heads." Thus, we "make up our minds," "change our minds," or are "in two minds" about something. One of the key attributes of the mind in this sense is that it is a private area in which no one but the owner has access. No one else can "know your mind." They can only know what we communicate or what they see through our actions. When we get certain results, we may ask ourselves, "what was I thinking," or according to the actions we display, others may in turn ask, "who do you think you are?"

Parents, grandparents, and other loved ones don't want their children to experience pain. I would say that is true for anyone who loves us, even as adults. It is with only good intentions that the phrase "don't get your hopes up" is expressed by others. But, if we never get our hopes up, or get hopeful, it is very difficult to move forward in life or in any endeavour.

So, let's start there. Get your hopes up. Know that the good life awaits you and that abundance in many areas is your birthright. It starts with acknowledging how we were programmed and rewriting that programming. There are several good places to find this information, but I'd like to offer to you the starting point I work with most. That is a psychometric profile. This is a quick "personality survey" that evaluates aspects of one's very individual personality to show where one's strengths are and areas in which one may choose to seek support. In other words, it helps us to see who it is we see ourselves to be.

PSYCHOMETRICS

I have been extremely fortunate to have been trained as a psychometric analyst by Raymond Walley, a leading expert in this field for over twenty years. From him, I have learnt that a personality survey gives us a complete unbiased view of the you who lives in your head. Through a time-limited, forced-choice, multiple-choice questionnaire, which is completed in less than ten minutes, the person will unconsciously reveal to us what their self-image is and how they behave in a number of different environments. After all, who better to ask about you than you? There is a sample survey at the back of this book.

THE HISTORY OF PSYCHOMETRIC PROFILING

In the early 1920s, the American psychologist William Moulton Marston developed a theory to explain people's emotional responses. Up until that time, work of this kind had mainly been confined to the mentally ill or criminally insane, but Marston wanted to extend these ideas to cover the personalities of ordinary individuals.

In order to test his theories, Marston needed some way of measuring the personalities he was trying to describe. His solution was to develop his own test to measure four important factors. The factors he chose were Dominance, Influence, Steadiness and Compliance, which gives us the DISC acronym.

In 1928, Marston published his findings in a book entitled, The Emotions of Normal People, which included a brief description of the test he had developed.

THE DEVELOPMENT OF DISC

In common with many similar tools (including the IQ test), DISC first came to prominence in the military – it was widely used as part of the US Army's recruitment process during the years leading to the Second World War. Having proved its value, it gradually came to be used in a more general recruitment setting.

Personality survey charts measure people using four factors – Dominance, Influence, Steadiness, and Compliance, and has a median line running horizontally across the center of the chart. Where a factor falls below this line, the indicated behaviour changes dramatically. Such changes simply indicate differences and not good or bad, positive or negative.

Psychometric analysis is complex, but a brief overview follows for your understanding. Of course, further explanations and examples will follow in subsequent chapters. At no stage do we ever refer to a person as being one dominating factor, as each set of charts vary and give you a broader picture of one's personality.

PERSONALITY SURVEY

The personality survey measures essential work-related aspects of an individual's behaviour including:

Motivational factors

Potential strengths

Potential weaknesses

Learning style

People skills

Management style

Sales and management potential

Potential to manage effectively

Potential as a team member

Potential as a team leader

Behaviour under pressure

Stress measurement.

Personality survey charts measure people using four factors – Dominance, Influence, Steadiness, and Compliance, and has a median line running horizontally across the center of the chart. Where a factor falls below this line, the indicated behaviour changes dramatically. Such changes simply indicate differences and not good or bad, positive or negative.

SCORE BOX

	D	i	S	C	BLANKS	TOTAL
MOST	⬭	⬡	⬯	⬠		
LEAST	◇	△	▢	☆		
DIFFERENCE						

Chart 1 – Difference	Chart 2 – Most	Chart 3 – Least
Basic behaviour	Potential work Behaviour	Probable behaviour under pressure

Chart 1 – Difference (Basic behaviour)

D	i	S	C
20	17	19	15
16	9	11	7
15	8	10	6
14	7	9	5
13		8	
12	6	7	4
10	5	5	3
9	4	4	2
8	3	3	1
7	2	2	0
5	1	1	-1
3	0	0	-2
0	-1	-2	-3
-2	-2	-3	-4
-3	-3	-4	-5
-4	-4	-5	-6
-6	-5	-6	-7
-7	-6	-7	-8
-9	-7	-8	-9
-10	-8	-9	-10
-11	-9	-10	-11
-13	-10	-11	-12
-14	-10	-12	
-21	-19	-19	-16

Chart 2 – Most (Potential work Behaviour)

D	i	S	C
20	17	19	15
16	10	12	9
15	9	11	8
14	8	10	7
12	7	9	
10	6	8	6
9		7	5
8	5	6	
7		5	4
6	4	4	3
5	3	3	
4		2	2
3	2	1	1
2	1	0	
1			
0	0	0	0

Chart 3 – Least (Probable behaviour under pressure)

D	i	S	C
0	0	0	0
		1	1
1	1	2	2
		3	3
2	2		
		4	4
3	3	5	5
4		6	6
	4		7
6	5	7	8
8			
9	6	8	9
10			
11	7	9	10
12	8	10	
13			11
14	9	11	
15	10		
16	11	12	12
		13	13
21	19	19	16

A brief overview follows for your understanding. Of course, further explanations and examples will follow in subsequent chapters. At no stage do we ever refer to a person as being one dominating factor, as each set of charts vary and give you a broader picture of one's personality.

A person whose major strength is high on the Dominance factor, for example, is one who we'd call a "driver." This person would be demanding, hard-driving, blunt, aggressive, and pushy. This person would be a director of people, whose nature is to command not ask. Their reason for action is, "What's in it for me?" They will have a tendency to see things in black and white, yes and no, and so are suspicious of grey areas. For them, power and control over their ability to affect their own destiny is all important. They most fear failure. These people make up about 10-15% of the population, and are often found in positions of power and strength.

A person whose major strength is high in Influence, such as myself, is an "expressive," is influential, persuasive (but can also be persuaded), verbal, noisy, enthusiastic, communicative, talkative, and usually highly empathetic. They can be likely to forget that they have two ears and one mouth, will genuinely like people, and subsequently have a strong need to be liked. People high in the "I" factor work hard to maintain harmony, and their major fear is rejection. Natural integrative leaders and people-orientated, they may ask, "How do you feel about that?" We make up about 20% of the population and are often found in sales positions.

Those whose major strength is a high "S" (Steadiness) are "amiables," and are reserved, steadfast, suspicious, thorough, stable, steady, reliable, tenacious and persistent. Amiable and easy-going, these people are trustworthy – the sort of person you'd trust on sight. Such people don't get angry; they get even. They are the social glue, and no company can survive without them since they are generally the people who make things work and run smoothly. Probably 50% of the population has this major factor as an element of their persona. Having a strong need to gather all the information and compare facts, these people will ask, "Why?" Their single most fear is insecurity. These people are the "power behind the throne," and see themselves as second-in-command. They are often found in positions such as personal assistants and secretaries.

If the major strength is a high "C" (Compliance) factor, this person is an "analytic." This person is good with words, accurate, precise, picky, pedantic, rule-orientated, logical, a perfectionist and law-abiding. They will know what is meant by elegant. For these people, knowledge is power; therefore, they will learn for the sake of learning, are often highly qualified, and can be in several diverse disciplines. Having high integrity, a person high on the "C" factor would never work in a company selling a product they do not believe in. An "analytic" will most fear disorder and confrontation, unless of course they believe they are right! They probably represent less than 10% of the population. These people are often found in highly technical roles. Interestingly, this can vary in different cultures.

Personality surveys can also be great indicators of the level of one's EQ (emotional intelligence), which Daniel Goleman says "plays a far greater role in thought, decision-making and individual success than is commonly acknowledged."

PERSONAL AND PERSONALITY

Since I am writing from my own personal experience, you will hear much about me and my path to success. I want to inspire you with my story and the obstacles I've overcome in the process. I want you to know, as I was told throughout my life, that you are wonderful. You are an artist.

Did you know that Einstein failed repeatedly? Isn't that surprising? He was unsuccessful at many attempts throughout his education and scientific career, and he wasn't considered by his teachers to be intelligent enough to further his higher education. Yet he is the standard by which we measure intellectual accomplishments. Think about what it means when one is called "Einstein." His name is now an adjective in the English language!

LIBERATE YOURSELF

Another great historical figure is Olaudah Equiano. Equiano was an 18th-century slave who paid what amounts to about £200,000 in today's figures to obtain his freedom. How did a slave do such a thing? How did a slave develop a self-image leading to a life of success? Sources dispute the birthplace of Olaudah. He was either born in Guinea - modern-day Nigeria - and sold into slavery as a child as his autobiography The Interesting Narrative of the Life of Olaudah Equiano or Gustavus Vassa, the African states, or he was born a slave in South Carolina during the colonial period of the United States about the year 1745. Slave narratives were beginning to become popular at the time, but rarely were they written personally by the slaves. Anyway, these slave narratives often included the birthplace stories of other slaves as a common theme in order to unite the experiences of all of the oppressed. Equiano, however, was sold to an officer in the British Royal Navy named Michael Paschal, around age ten, or circa 1755. Paschal renamed him Gustavus Vassa after an historical Swedish hero and king who liberated the Swedes from Danish oppression during the 16th century. Whatever Paschal's motives were for renaming Equiano, it seems that setting forth this intention worked out well for Equiano, but not without much due diligence.

Equiano served as Paschal's steward on board naval vessels and was ultimately forced to fight during wartime. Paschal sent Equiano to school in London, where he learned to read and write. He was able to apply much of this learning in traveling the world with Paschal, though still in bondage and servitude to his owner. Since he was a baptized Christian and a sailor for the British, he felt that he was due some of the spoils of war. In other words, he wanted to be paid, but Paschal refused to compensate his slave from the windfall he earned in sea battle. Paschal suddenly sold his royally-named slave to another sea captain, who then sold him to another man, a Quaker, Robert King. The good thing about Quakers is that they are, and were, very peaceful people, so mistreatment of slaves would have been anathema. King, (and isn't it ironic that the king works for the king?) trained him as a gauger, someone who gauges weights and measurements, which was a very responsible position requiring education and skill. A businessman would know better than to waste such an educated individuals' talents and skills by putting him in the fields of a plantation, so this seemed quite proper. After three years in this position in finance, Equiano saved enough to buy his freedom for £40.

Equiano went back to sea as a hairdresser and steward. (Remember the powder wigs popular at the time for men? A bit like what high court judges still wear today.) He eventually joined the very famous British explorer Horatio Nelson in Nelsons' explorations to find a northwest passage to India. What an accomplished man, even by today's standards! He later married a British woman and published his book. It was hugely successful, as the onset of the abolitionist movement had begun to eradicate slavery worldwide. He even became involved with political and legal efforts regarding this horrid practice.

So, this story of Olaudah Equiano is indeed inspiring and uplifting, but so what? Well, what sort of self-image do you think Equiano had? Obviously he did not feel trapped by the restraints of his time for slaves. I've no doubt that Equiano felt the bondage under which he served, but it didn't stop him. He found the way to achieve the goal he most desired – FREEDOM! This was very much affected by his ability to create financial wealth, and therefore influence.

Most of you reading this today do not have the literal bonds of slavery holding you back, but perhaps you have some other type of programming keeping you "tied" to a way of life. Let's take inspiration from Olaudah Equiano, whose self-image, education, personality, and drive liberated not only him, but enabled him to begin work that would eventually outlaw slavery.

I would like to note here that slavery still exists in many parts of the world. It is a practice that not only keeps humans in substandard, deplorable living and working arrangements, but it also keeps the slave "owners" in a position of scarcity, lack and an overall poverty mindset. Our focus here should be on liberating ourselves so as to put ourselves in positions where we can positively affect others. When we can influence by example, like Olaudah Equiano and countless others, whose liberation from literal bondage was not only an inspiration to other slaves, but helped to change the minds of people who wholeheartedly believed that Africans were sub-human and therefore incapable of equal intellect to that of Caucasians.

Another superb example of modern-day liberation is Oprah. Though she was not a slave, she faced the very real issue of racist and sexist ideas of a person's place in society. She uses her influence as a successful individual to inspire and motivate underprivileged people of all races and sexes. Rest assured that your own personal successes can and do serve the greater good when achieved in the right ways and for positive reasons.

MOTIVATION

According to philosopher Bob Proctor, "No successful person who ever accomplished anything knew how they were going to do it; they just knew that they would." Proctor, an incredibly influential philosopher and featured speaker of the hit DVD The Secret, businessman and Life Coach artist, was told he shouldn't even attempt to go to college! He was told by teachers that he was better off in a trade school after his secondary education was complete. His teachings regarding creating the life you want include the idea that you must first have a desire to accomplish something. Figuring out what it is that you want to achieve is an early step on the path to financial success.

Another amazing tool I use when working with many clients is the Structured Interview which examines important elements of emotional intelligence (EQ) such as self-responsibility, self-insight, self-development and maturity. Part of the structured interview is a Sales Aptitude Indicator which reveals one's desire for material success, and indeed, one's ability in a sales situation. Knowing your mind, your personality, and most importantly, having a desire are very helpful in determining what you want.

Bob Proctor shows us how to have abundance in all areas of life, and how to create a life full of wonder and amazement. I'm always amazed, too, that he is very willing to not only show us how to achieve these wonderful things in life and to assure us that we too can achieve fabulous things, but he also shares with his students where his teachings came from. In other words, Proctor tells us who his teachers are and were. He refers to himself still, as a student of himself. He says, "I've been studying me for over 40 years." Part of this study of self includes knowing how one sees him or herself, and adapting that self to be the best possible individual that one can be. Psychometric analysis helps us find out what that programming is, how it reflects in our self-image, and how to channel it into the goals we would like to achieve.

My friends, I want you to know that life is a journey and your path can take you in any direction you choose. Choose a good one! Choose one full of beauty, abundance, family, friends and joy!

So, I asked you about your self-image. What thoughts did that invoke? Did you immediately go to something positive or negative? Did you think, "I am kind and generous – I am the 21st century 'Good Samaritan,'" or did something negative pop up? Did you immediately think about your size, poor choices of three years or three months or 30 years ago? Did you think, "I'd be lovely if only I could lose three kilograms," or "I'm not bad looking if it weren't for this scar, this blemish," or any other negative aspect of your physical appearance? First, I'd like to say you are beautiful the way you are, but if you want to change your physical appearance or health, the ideas in this book for success in life are 100% applicable to outward image without the necessity for plastic surgery or radical changes from what nature gave you at birth. Changing our self-image is changing how we see who we are, starting with the inside. When we change the image of ourselves in our minds, then the outward appearance changes on its own. Embrace your beauty that only you have. Even if you are an identical twin, your beauty is your own. As you digest each chapter in this book and apply it to your life and your special journey of artistry and greatness, your beauty will come forth like a rainbow after a dark storm. You will learn to see yourself in new expressive forms.

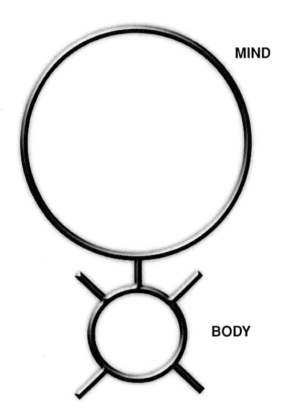

MIND

BODY

THE STICK PERSON

Here is another helpful tool for me to help explain how your thoughts affect how you see yourself, and this tool will also help you to see how your thoughts manifest concrete things in your exterior world. This is the "stick person" concept.

The stick person concept was developed by Dr. Thurman Fleet, founder of the concept therapy movement in the early 1930s, He was a chiropractor, and felt that in order to heal his patients holistically – in other words, the entire body and mind – he must give them a clear image of the mind. His belief was that we think in pictures, and without a clear image of the mind, the patient would have nothing to work with.

Here is an example of what Dr. Fleet meant by thinking in pictures. If I asked you to think of your house, a picture of your house will run across the screen of your mind. The same will happen for anything to which you are emotionally attached. From this, Dr. Fleet developed a drawing in which the head is noticeably larger than the body, suggesting that our mind has dominance over our body, and not the reverse as many would believe.

For most people, all conscious attention is on their physical body and physical results, when in fact, everything we experience in our body is an expression of our mind. Since your mind is an activity and not your physical brain, it is important to have a clear picture of what your mind looks like.

Following Dr. Thurman Fleet's example of the stick person, the process is thus: for simplicity, let's split our mind into two main parts – the conscious mind and the subconscious mind. Our conscious mind is our thinking mind; it is where we can accept, reject or neglect any idea which comes into our mind, but we use only a small percentage of our conscious mind.

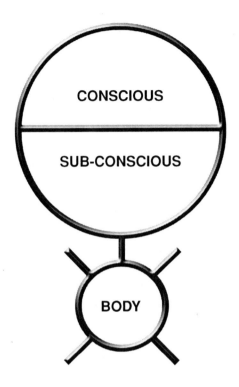

SUBCONSCIOUS MIND

Shakespeare, one of history's most prolific and profound creative writers, and certainly an artiste extraordinaire, wrote about the processes of the mind,

"…But then begins the journey in my head
To work my mind, when body's work's expir'd;
For then my thoughts, from far where I abide,
Intend a zealous pilgrimage to thee,
And keep my drooping eyelids open wide. . ."

William Shakespeare's Sonnet XXVII

Our subconscious mind is our emotional mind, and regulates all bodily sensations, such as taste, touch, sight, hearing and smell. These senses are hard-wired to our brain, and they are things which we do not need to think about. Here in our subconscious mind is also where our habits are formed. The subconscious mind has no ability to reject an idea; it simply accepts every suggestion made to it. Most of us are familiar with the playfulness and uninhibited nature of hypnotic subjects; simply by tapping into the subconscious mind, the behaviours displayed are seemingly different than the person's "normal" personality, as they have no ability during hypnosis to consciously think of the actions they display.

The subconscious is also where our memories are stored. Our self-image is made up of memories which have an emotional connection to the past and cannot serve us when attempting to break old habits. The subconscious mind is the sum total of our past experiences. What we feel, think, or do forms the basis of our experience.

Experiences are stored in the form of subtle impressions in our subconscious mind. These impressions interact with one another and give birth to tendencies. We become prone to react in a particular way to a particular situation or stimulus depending upon the tendencies in our subconscious mind. The result of these tendencies determines our character. The subconscious mind is always working – it's the motor of the brain; it is what allows us to know and do things instinctively.

We know from neuroscience that thought produces chemical reactions in our brain, which affects our physical body by changing the way we feel. What we believe in our subconscious mind (our emotional mind) is what we feel and is expressed through our actions. Our actions are what give us our results. So if you want to know what you are thinking subconsciously, simply look at your results. If you want to change the results you are getting, you need to change what you think about. Most people look at their results as their potential. This is not accurate. The results we have been getting up until now are merely a reflection of our past thoughts. Once we learn to paint beautiful pictures in our mind of what we now want, our results will reflect that.

"Behaviour is the mirror in which everyone shows their image."

Johann Wolfgang Von Goethe

MENTAL FACULTIES

There are six mental faculties as discussed in Napoleon Hill's classic book Think and Grow Rich.

MEMORY is the ability to store, retain, and subsequently recall information. What we choose to store in our memory of ourselves, and that which we maintain an emotional connection with, is what amounts to our self-image. We can choose to remember all of our past successes, which ultimately will keep us striving for further success, or we can dwell on situations which have not gone so favourably for us, and ultimately paralyse any efforts we make to move forward. This can be changed, however, by holding new pictures in our mind of who we are, who we aspire to be, and who we deserve to be. We can list all of our successes, no matter how small they may seem, and choose to dwell on those in order to feel successful. We can hold an image of one of our heroes or heroines and all the amazing attributes they possess. We can picture ourselves in new surroundings and enjoy the emotion of actually being there now. This is where our imagination comes into play.

IMAGINATION Some psychologists have preferred to describe this process as "imaging" or "imagery." Imagined images are seen with the "mind's eye." Albert Einstein reportedly stated that "imagination is more important than knowledge." It is imagination which has brought us to this stage technologically and in every other way imaginable. Excuse the pun.

"Everyone visualizes, whether he knows it or not.
Visualizing is the great secret of success."

Genevieve Behrend

Perception is another important factor. As a single mother for many years, my perception of my situation was one of embarrassment, and maybe even to some extent regret for being unwed. I've since changed that view of myself, I'm glad to say, and have come to recognise my many strengths in raising three sons single-handedly. I now celebrate the role they each play in my life. Author Dr. Wayne Dyer wrote, "when you change the way you look at things, the things you look at change." How true I have found that to be. It brings to mind the old adage of looking at a glass of water and perceiving it as being half empty or half full. The only thing we ever need to change is our perception of how we view ourselves, others and the things around us. I've had so many wonderful teachers who have shown me how to improve my perception. Charles Bentley, Ph.D., says, "If we try to change ourselves, we'll fail. If we try to change others, we'll fail, but if we change our perception of who we are – that's the only real change."

WILL Most of us are familiar with the concept of "free will." It is often discussed in our early religious or spiritual upbringing, or even simply when parents, guardians and teachers discuss our behaviours with us in early childhood. One has choices! The definition of the "will," according to the Webster's dictionary is:

1.   The capability of conscious choice, decision and intention;

2.   A fixed and persistent intent or purpose.

One's will is one's ability to concentrate, to focus on a single thing and not be distracted by anything else going on. As Bob Proctor says, "The will is to the mind what a magnifying glass is to the sun." It is like focusing the same energy which gives us light onto a sheet of paper and watching the sun burn a hole through it. Our will drives our mind. It allows us to move forward with our perceptions, and especially our self-image. The will is what makes us get out of bed each morning to either dread or face the new day with enthusiasm. Since one has the ability to choose how to embrace the day, that is a very good place to start and put into practice how to change self-perception. Simply choose to see the new day as glorious and full of possibilities for success and greatness. Even if you aren't enthused about going to work or school or wherever else you must venture, start by practicing what it feels like to be enthused about your day and you'll soon find that your day is something to be enthused about.

Our **INTUITION** is when we are correct about an inspired feeling without knowing why. It is something which happens instinctively. Intuition is linked with intent; it is the bridge between the conscious and the unconscious. Some people seem to have a more developed intuition than others. Many people trust "women's intuition" or "a mother's intuition," but this phenomenon is not limited to those of us fortunate enough to have been born female. We all get inspired thoughts regarding the necessary or appropriate course of action. Women may have a more developed sense of their intuition simply because we have been conditioned to anticipate impending situations regarding our offspring or other persons in our care, and we instinctively act upon these instincts. Or maybe, just maybe, our intuition has developed more profoundly in some cases because we were told we have this gift, therefore we see it as true about ourselves. It is part of our self-image.

> Intuition is linked with intent; it is the bridge between the conscious and the unconscious.

We can also use our intuition wrongly. If we are used to getting average results and suddenly get an idea of how we can gain outstanding results and earn vast sums of money, we may allow the opportunity to pass and justify our actions by telling ourselves that it probably wouldn't have worked anyway. The truth is that we would never have thought of the idea if we were not capable of achieving it. In situations such as this, the only question we need ask is, "Will this idea take me in the direction of my dreams?" If the answer is "yes," you must act on it immediately.

REASON is part of our human experience. It is not wholly dependent upon schooling, but often schooling can affect it and not always positively. Philosophers and scientists throughout history have used reasoning in order to better the human or life experience, or at least attempt to improve the quality of life for society. Reasoning is something which we do with our conscious mind rather than our subconscious mind. It is the method which employs logic; thus, it raises our knowledge from the perceptual level, which we share with animals, to the conceptual level, which sets us apart from the animal kingdom. Aristotle called man "the rational animal" because it is the reasoning faculty that most distinguishes us from other creatures, but we do not reason automatically. Aristotle was one of the first scientists to develop a scientific process known as Aristotelian Logic or "deductive reasoning." Whereas this process is no longer what we use in scientific research, Aristotle paved the way for us to develop our reasoning abilities and apply logic to the universe around us. Humans began more efficiently to explore the universe around them, how it affects them, and how they affect the universe.

We have free will, and we are fallible. This is why we first need knowledge. We must know ourselves or our mind. Through psychometric analysis you can find a path to begin the magnificent journey toward

> Aristotle called man "the rational animal" because it is the reasoning faculty that most distinguishes us from other creatures

health, happiness, wealth and creativity that many of us desire. Know that it cannot completely change one's basic character; however, new behaviours can be taught. We recommend that an individual completes a survey twice a year, as changes in the home or working environment can have an effect on the personality. It also enables us to motivate you in a manner appropriate for you as an individual and understand why you may do things in a certain way. We must recognise our programming and understand that how we see ourselves may be the result of negative programming and therefore is not the "truth." We can change our programming by understanding how we've been conditioned. We can reprogram or condition the mind by using tools, laws and exercises, and the imagination to awaken the mind to something more powerful than you imagined.

PROMISE

Promise Yourself

To be so strong that nothing can disturb your peace of mind.

To talk health, happiness, and prosperity to every person you meet.

To make all your friends feel that there is something worthwhile in them.

To look at the sunny side of everything and make your optimism come true.

To think only of the best, to work only for the best and to expect only the best.

To be just as enthusiastic about the success of others as you are about your own.

To forget the mistakes of the past and press on to the greater achievements of the future.

To wear a cheerful expression at all times and give a smile to every living creature you meet.

To give so much time to improving yourself that you have no time to criticize others.

To be too large for worry, too noble for anger, too strong for fear, and too happy to permit the presence of trouble.

To think well of yourself and to proclaim this fact to the world, not in loud word, but in great deeds.

To live in the faith that the whole world is on your side, so long as you are true to the best that is in you.

Christian D. Larson

Chapter Two

You Weren't Born Rich? So What?

Chapter Two

You Weren't Born Rich? So What?

We often become comfortable making excuses for why we can't be successful. One may replay failures or obstacles we faced in our minds for decades. Many people place blame on others for their lack of success. Focusing on the trials of our past lives will only hold us back. It keeps us stuck in the past and recreates the same results for our future. It limits our view of the world and ourselves, and then we really are stuck. But we're only immobile until we change our perception of things. We must change this perception; then our self-image changes and we can then affect our future. So, what limits our future is the same thing that allows us to bring about change for our future. How we see ourselves is how we effectively change our future. It is that simple.

Today even less fortunate children tend to have much more regulated schedules, but that was not my experience growing up. The children of my neighbourhood were "latch key" kids after school hours, and played outdoors in what would today be considered a very dangerous atmosphere. Our parents and caretakers thought that our play times were as innocent as theirs may have been growing up, but this was where I first became aware of the many goings on in the criminal underworld. In some ways I think that the faith of my guardians protected me, but unfortunately many of my neighbourhood friends were not so fortunate. I can only think of a few of them who did not get involved in drugs and crime.

Though I feel blessed to have survived and excelled in life, I have often wondered why I escaped the tempting lure of class A drugs, for instance. Was it as simple as being told I was wonderful, so I had no need to find that place of acceptance one finds from participating in such behaviours? Was it because my grandparents continually told me I was great and I could achieve anything? Or was it my own self-image? If it is my self-image, then one can definitely see that the language and communication from those who loved me affected that.

GROWING UP

I was born December 30, 1972, in Lambeth Hospital, London. 43 Chessington House, Union Road, London, became my home for the next five years. The estate I lived on was culturally diverse; it was an old council estate very similar to housing projects in the United States where everyone knew everyone else, no matter their age or background. There was a sense of community and everyone looked out for one another. People would knock at their neighbour's flat for a cup of sugar. As children, we would go to the shop for the older people in the flats and be rewarded with 10 or 20 pence.

I always felt at home there and safe; it was all I knew. I lived in a four-bedroom flat on the top floor with my mother, grandparents, two aunts, two uncles and a cousin. I did say it was cramped, did I not? My grandparents, however, were Jamaican immigrants and this lifestyle of extended family living together was not uncommon in the culture from which they came. My cousin was four years my senior and was being raised by my grandparents. His mother died twenty one months before I was born under very suspicious circumstances; there was talk of murder, but no evidence supported this. Therefore, the man our family suspected of killing her was never brought to trial. Stories of my deceased 19-year-old aunt were always being told by my grandparents, so that it almost felt she was still there with us. Family, whether present or not, were very important to us.

In our household, we didn't have the luxury of the things I have at my disposal today. We had a small black and white television, and the picture would jump so it was hard to follow anything that you watched. Our electricity supply came from a slot meter, which would always cut out before someone remembered to top it up. There was no running hot water or central-heating, so we would go to a local shop to buy paraffin for a small heater that we'd all huddle around in the living room. Each of us would take turns washing using a small bowl beside the paraffin heater whilst attempting to get more warm than clean. Most of the surrounding community was quite poor, but we seemed more overcrowded than the others. During school holidays, all of my cousins would stay with my grandparents, making the situation even tighter.

Baths, if they happened, would be once a week on a Sunday morning straight after cornmeal porridge and fried dumplings, which my grandmother would make into favourite shapes for us all.

Sunday mornings were almost a celebration. My grandmother would sing and play the tambourine and get us to bang pot lids and boxes as a way of joining in the fun. It was the only morning when we didn't have toast and hot chocolate for breakfast so that, if nothing else, was definitely something to celebrate.

My mother had gone back to work as an audio typist when I was three months old, and from that point my grandparents became my parents. It felt as though my mother was there to pay for school dinners, school journeys and new clothes. She left too early to take me to school, and was working when school plays were on. I was an extremely shy child, and usually took parts that did not have lines, but my mother's attendance would have been thrilling for me. She would get home from work too late to collect me from school.

We would go on a big shopping trip to Clapham Junction once a year and she was proud to announce that she'd spent £100 on new clothes for me. My shoes were always tighter than they should have been throughout the year, leaving me with crooked toes, our family trademark. I don't have any early memories of Christmas, though I can always remember loving that time of year. It would snow every year, and I loved the silence of snowy mornings. There is such an element of peace that comes with the quietude of a snowy day.

I took a lot of time off school as I suffered with everything, from boils to tonsillitis. On snowy days, however, I'd be the first person through the school gates. I continued to live in Chessington House until I was five, when one day my mother had a chance meeting with a young divorced Jewish man who knocked on our door to offer his services as a photographer. He had one daughter who was the same age as me, and he would bring her round on the weekend. In order to get his subjects to smile, he would ask them to say "nicky nacky noow." Unbeknownst to my stepsister, this was the nickname my family had given her. She'd always want to play childish or "girlie" games. I was used to playing with a much older male cousin, so I found it hard to "dumb down" as I saw it.

Soon after meeting my first stepfather, my mother decided that she was happy to take the relationship more seriously with her new love. They decided they would move in together and I was to come along, too. I wasn't keen on this idea, but I was happy that as we would be living only five minutes away in Knebworth House, I could still see my grandparents every day before and after school. This was the first time that I had my own bedroom, and I would give my mum hell every night pretending I'd seen a ghost or heard a bump in the night – playing on the many ghost stories my grandmother would tell us of her paranormal experiences back in Jamaica.

> This was the first time that I had my own bedroom, and I would give my mum hell every night pretending I'd seen a ghost or heard a bump in the night.

I'd been attending Larkhall Nursery School for the first two years of my part-time education, and now it was time for me to start school full-time. Larkhall was seen as a 'bad' school locally, but it was all I knew and even though I had a lot of time off, I was still one of the brightest pupils in the class.

TALL DARK STRANGER

One sunny day, I remember there being a knock at the door. A tall, slim black man and short white woman walked in. Everything seemed to fall silent. My mother said, "Debbii, this is your dad." I was over the moon; at last I had a dad. It opened up new hopes of having a man other than my grandfather telling me how wonderful I was and how great I was going to be when I grew up. Grandad was great. He spoiled us and would let us have a sip of Sanatogen, a tonic wine drunk by many West Indian people which he kept under his bed, but he was old and walked slowly. Now, this mystery man, my "dad," was everything I'd dreamt of having. Somehow I had to contain my excitement as I didn't want to disappoint my mother. I always remember her complaining that my dad "had run off and left us." My mother, wanting to show off how bright I was to my father, asked me to write my name for him. As I wrote Debbie McKoy on the sheet of paper, I recall a strange look on his face, as though he'd expected my name to be Debbie Lee, which is his surname. This child's intuition proved accurate as I only recently learned that he sees my use of McKoy as my surname as me rejecting my "proper name."

After that, I would write letters to my father and soon started flying to visit him and his wife at his home in Germany. My early visits to Germany opened my eyes to new possibilities, and it gave me new aspirations for the future. My father lived in a nice home which was clean, organised and clutter-free. He had many books and would always stress the importance of reading. At Christmas time, he had a Christmas tree, we would exchange presents which we'd open on Christmas Eve, and we'd eat Christmas dinner together around the dining table. Although my mother's husband was self-employed, earned a good living and was from a middle-class Jewish family, life was nothing like this at home. Having been in the British Army and based in Germany since he was 16, my father had a very prim and proper way about him. He was always well-groomed, and carried himself in a very upright manner. I admired the fact that he spoke German so fluently; he was my "dad." However, he was as strict as a convent nun and gave me no leeway for being his only child who he'd just met. I don't know if this was partly the reason why I found it so difficult to call him "dad." It just didn't roll off the tongue the way that "mummy," "nanny," or "grandad" did. Dad's wife, my step-mum, was always a kind, loving, gentle and affectionate lady. She made efforts to teach me some German even when my father refused to do so. I admire her for staying with my father all of these years as she was with him when he fathered me, and she even stayed with him when he fathered my younger sister. All she's said is that that was a trying time. I'm sure it was! I only found out about my sister nine years ago; she is now 23. On a visit to Germany, my father took me to her house and said, "I'm sure you can guess who that is?" My heart sank. Up until that point, I thought I was his only child. My life has been full of surprises!

At home with my mother, things became unsettled, and I can recall her telling her husband how low she was feeling, almost on a daily basis. He would always reply coldly to "snap out of it," and wouldn't pay much attention to her emotional state. They were arguing as often as her emotional down days. On one occasion, the argument became so heated that my mother told her husband to get out, and as she slammed the front door behind him her arm smashed through the glass in the door. I'd never seen that much blood before. I was hysterical and convinced that my mother was about to die. Mum's death or the possibility of it was one of my greatest fears, as it is for most young children. She was rushed to the hospital where she received seven stitches in her arm. I was whisked round to my grandparents.

THE BIG WIN

Then my grandad won the "pools," which are gambling pots on soccer games. It was enough to take our minds off my mother's depression for a while. My grandad had been playing the pools for quite some time. He claimed that he would dream winning numbers, and, being a man of strong faith, he would play every week in one of his six children's names in the knowledge that he would win. My grandad was a devout Christian, and would walk the local streets shouting "repent," and "dem a go burn" at the top of his voice in his thick Jamaican accent. As a Christian convert to the Seventh Day Adventist Church, Grandad was obsessed with the "End Times" as prophesied in the Book of Revelations.

He felt it his mission to warn non-believers to the coming apocalypse. But this doesn't mean he let go of all of his traditional Jamaican beliefs! We were often concerned that someone cursed us or had the potential to do so. Spells or curses could be cast with any items from a person. We burned the hair that came from our brushes, for example, in order to prevent foes from attacking us spiritually. Knickers were seen as especially potent carriers of one's essence, and we each washed our own to prevent anyone else from claiming them for ill intent. So, the idea that Grandad legitimately dreamt of the winning numbers was easy for us to believe!

When the win of £58,000 eventually came in 1980, it was the best and worst thing to ever happen to my family all at the same time. None of us had ever seen that much money before and suddenly there was a gold rush. Everyone was squabbling over who should get what and why. With her share, my mother paid money toward the mortgage of the house she had recently bought in Croydon with her husband. My uncle bought a house not too far away in Thornton Heath and there was talk of it being a "better area." All I noticed was that there were fewer blacks and so became slightly suspicious of my mothers' intentions.

MENTAL ILLNESS

By the time we moved into our new house, things worsened for my mother. She would tell me how she was hearing voices to kill herself. Being alone in the house with my mother most of the time, I was scared to go to school or go out to play as most seven-year-olds would, in case I came back to find her dead. In the morning, I would iron my school uniform, make breakfast for us both, and then go off to Elmwood School, which was a short walk away on Lodge Road.

When I returned home from school, I would make dinner for both myself and my mother, since by this time she was sleeping a lot, had put on loads of weight, had slowed down tremendously, and couldn't do much to help herself. Whenever my mother's husband was home, I can only remember a feeling of discomfort in the house. Soon it came to light that he'd been having an affair with another black single mother whom he'd met much in the same way that he did my mother, by knocking on her door and offering his services as a photographer. The strange thing was that when he first started dating my mother and announced to his family his intention of marrying her, they disowned him because of her being black. To my knowledge, they never welcomed him back. I think my mother took this willingness to lose one's family as a sign of sacrifice and true love. Yet here he was doing the same thing again. It was surely a crushing blow to her personally and might have affected her concept of love overall. I certainly see where it probably adversely affected my ideas on love. As a child and young adult, I never wanted to get married or have children. I seemed to attract rejection from the boys I liked, so love was not something I focused on. I know now that love is a wonderful experience and I feel worthy of it. I no longer feel the need to attract rejection on any level from any human being. I understand that humans do not always share the same tastes, and I know that I am lovable and beautiful. But it took a long time for me to truly understand this.

I started to become a misfit; I was too "black" in Croydon, and too "white" in Union Grove. People would say I spoke posh..

Beginning divorce proceedings pushed my mother even further into deterioration, so it was decided that I should go to live with my grandparents again. Though I was worried about leaving my mother by herself, I was happy that I was going back to my old school and the area where I felt most at home. The novelty soon wore off though. Maybe I'd seen too much of a change, and the contrast between the life I had and the life I'd come back to was too great. I started to become a misfit; I was too "black" in Croydon, and too "white" in Union Grove. People would say I spoke posh, and I would do everything in my power to try to sound more "street." I felt so trapped in my situation, and nobody I knew could even begin to understand what I was going through. I was just seen as a pretty little spoilt only child whose father was rich (which he wasn't) and lived in Germany. Having seen the disruption that my grandfathers' winnings had caused the family, I started to become obsessed with the idea of becoming a millionaire and putting things right. I felt that if I got rich enough, I'd fit in with everyone. From that point on, I was on a mission.

My mother received her decree absolute to say that her divorce was final, and it was a happy time. She was recovering in leaps and bounds, and was working full-time again. We had a new flat, and my mother had a new boyfriend. Then, she found out she was pregnant – just when I felt I was finally getting my mother back, as she had told me that it was our time now. I was devastated. Where or when was it my time with her? I felt it was a ploy to replace me, the "bad news from the past." During my mother's initial recovery, she would carry a picture of my cousin's sister, a pretty mixed-race girl, in her bag and would tell people that she was her daughter. With her being pregnant by a white man, it made me feel that this was all she had ever wanted, and that she felt I was a mistake. I think a part of me died at that point. I felt left out and even further pushed out when she suggested I should go to stay with my aunt for the duration of her pregnancy. All sorts of memories came flooding back. My uncle's wife once told me that when they were out with me when I was a baby, she would say that I was her niece. I think this was an attempt by my uncle's now ex-wife to prove to herself that she was a better mother than mine, which may have been true at the time, but it was still a mean-spirited comment to tell a child. Now all I had was my aunt who I was staying with, my grandparents, and hip-hop.

HIP-HOP – MY FIRST LOVE

Hip-hop was my only love. It provided me the escape I needed. It took me to a place where everyone loved me and where blackness was something to be celebrated. I could be the beautiful young black woman who excelled. I fit in. I could "act black," and be accepted and even admired! I was great at this "black life" and that's a good thing, because I am black. I found my inner beauty. When I did that, the rest of the world could see my beauty as well.

My life had been one where my racially mixed family produced relatives who didn't necessarily look much like me, but about whom they boasted. I was much darker than many of my cousins and siblings. I had Auntie's comment and the picture of the lighter child haunting me like one of Nan's ghosts from Jamaica! I would stay awake most of the night, searching the radio airwaves for anything that remotely sounded like a rap song. I rented the "learn how to break dance" video from the local video shop night after night. I would watch the local boys practicing all their latest moves on the roof in our estate. I quickly became one of the best "poppers," and friends of the family would pay me to dance at every event from shop openings to birthday parties. One night whilst driving home in my mother's new husband's car, he had the radio tuned into the Tim Westwood rap show on Capital Radio. I'm sure it was a complete fluke, and he just happened to have the radio tuned in, but I never before enjoyed my journey home so much. Though I doubt this was an expression of his love for me, perhaps he saw the joy he could bring to me. He was the best stepfather he could be, but he wasn't black and he couldn't identify with my newfound identity.

Yet this felt like déjà vu. My mother had a new man, she bought a house out of the area with him – this time in Mitcham, only now I had a baby brother 11 years my junior. Babies naturally get a lot of attention which isn't quite as freely given to a pre-teen girl.

I went to a couple of new schools, as the schooling system was different in that borough, which made the transition even more disruptive than it needed to be, but I still didn't feel like I fit in. I would go to school in the morning to register, then come back home to watch school and college programmes, and read encyclopedias all day. I'd then go back to school for last registration so nobody would know that I hadn't been at school all day. I soon became sloppy, and the only conversation anyone ever wanted to have with me was to question why since I was so intelligent, why didn't I want to attend school? By this point, I only ever wanted to go back to Union Grove to my aunt's flat on weekends and holidays, and my mother soon suggested I should go to live there.

My aunt, who is twelve years older than me, was always the cool one. She'd take me shopping with her and, let's say, 'obtain' new clothes for me when I was young. She would take me ice skating at the Streatham ice rink every Friday night with all of her cool friends. She had the latest fashions and a lovely flat, but now she had become a devout Jehovah's Witness and a single mother of one daughter. It was fun when I would visit on weekends, but now she became so strict and moany.

My thoughts turned to money as the only way I could see to escape this new trap. When I was in Mitcham, I had a paper round and would wash cars. That skill wasn't easily transferable on a council estate, so I had to get thinking. I decided that I would put advertisements in all of the news agents shop windows along Wandsworth Road to advertise my services as a babysitter. I struck gold! I was babysitting every night, and I also got a part-time job in a shoe shop on Oxford Street. Though my mother bought one good quality pair of shoes for me every year for my birthday, this did further my passion for quality footwear. Money was coming in from all directions, but I was still having late night thoughts of how I was going to become a millionaire by the time I reached my 18th birthday.

I could never face the thought of school after the sleepless nights, so would leave out in the morning and go back home once I knew my aunt had left for work. When my aunt found out that I was skipping school, she immediately made it clear that I could no longer live there. Where was I to go? My grandparents felt that they were too old to cope with any stress, my mother didn't want me back, and so the inevitable happened. I ended up in a children's home.

So, I wasn't born rich either. I faced many obstacles growing up that drove my childhood friends to crime, drug use and early death. But I am living proof that no matter what obstacles one faces in life, they can be overcome with drive, determination, a positive self-image, and pursuing a purpose in life that is fulfilling. We don't all like the same things and we aren't all blessed to be a black female who excels at hip-hop, but there is something out there that will bring you joy, help you see your own beauty, and achieve the successes of your wildest dreams.

THE BIG BOYS AND GIRLS

My story of emerging from this sort of life isn't unique. Many of today's most successful black entrepreneurs had less than privileged upbringings but found a way to develop the artist in them. A great example is Russell Simmons, founder of record label Def Jam and many other creative and philanthropic endeavors, who grew up in a middle-class neighbourhood in Queens, New York, that was crumbling due to the influx of crime and drugs. Though his biography says that he did dabble in small-time drug sales, he quickly learned this was not how he was going to excel in life. He took an idea, one small inspired thought, to promote a new and growing style of music.

In 1977, after attending a party at a small club where an MC was shouting out call-and-response rhymes over a break beat, Russell decided to promote parties featuring hip-hop artists. "I didn't have any talent," Russell says candidly, "so the only way to really be involved was to produce and promote....I loved the music. I was more passionate about the culture and the phenomenon that was developing in the community than I was in the actual business."

I certainly disagree with Simmons' comment that he had no talent. He is indeed an artist as we described in chapter one. He is one of the richest men in his industry and is considered the "Godfather of Hip-hop." Rap pioneer "Run" of Run DMC is his baby brother, too. In Russell Simmons' biography we hear that he quit his college education to pursue his passion, but there were no inspiring philanthropists and entrepreneurs who guided him. In fact, he says of his early days promoting musical acts that, "The only entrepreneurs we

> I was more passionate about the culture and the phenomenon that was developing in the community than I was in the actual business.

knew were the numbers guys and the drug dealers. And that's a fact. It was the only way in." He found his passion, or purpose, celebrated the culture and expression of his and other black communities, and stayed true to his desire to promote what brought him joy – hip-hop and rap. Russell Simmons' résumé includes many more business ventures too numerous to list here. His professional life is astounding, but he seems to know what really matters.

Although Russell is focused on success in the business world, he is also concerned with giving back in order to help the less fortunate and to improve urban communities. He started the Rush Philanthropic Arts Foundation in 1995, which provides disadvantaged youth with access to the arts. He also founded the Hip-Hop Summit Action Network in 2001, an organization that mixes political rallies with music concerts in order to register young voters.

There's more. After Hurricane Katrina, he organized an industry-wide foundation to help with victims of this disaster in New Orleans and the Mississippi Gulf Coast. Many areas devastated by the storm and subsequent floods due to the compromised levee systems were poverty-stricken black communities with little resources to initiate obtaining basic necessities, much less rebuilding homes, churches, schools, and businesses. Simmons is very in touch with the plight of the black community throughout the world, and he generously gives to those in need. How very profound to give back to the people whose patronage was only a small part of his overall success.

Another obvious, hugely successful business person and philanthropist is Oprah Winfrey. She grew up in the racially segregated southern United States during the Civil Rights movement. During Oprah's life she faced many obstacles, including racism and sexism, but she went on to be the youngest television news anchor in the United States, broadcasting the local Memphis, Tennessee news while she still in high school. She was the first black female in such a position as well. Imagine the difficulties of this position for a young woman.

But who doesn't know Oprah's name now? In fact, that we associate her by her first name only is indicative that she has achieved a sort of greatness, like one might say, "the queen" or "the Pope." To rattle off a list of her multi-billion dollar business ventures and charity contributions would take much space and possibly insult the reader. She is **one** of the most recognized faces in the world, too. She embraces what **it means** to be an artist, a woman and black. My point here is that she was not **born** rich, nor did she accomplish her success by someone handing it to her. Her entire purpose in life seems to be helping others find their joy in order to better their lives. What a purpose! What a woman!

Another of my favorite rap industry artists is Jay-Z, a professional name he developed from a nickname given to him by friends in his housing project in the Bronx, New York, where he grew up. Abandoned at age two by his father, Jay-Z, whose real name is Shawn Corey Carter, attended but didn't finish high school with some other big names in the music industry such as The Notorious B.I.G. and Busta Rhymes. From such a humble beginning, Jay-Z is now the second richest rap artist. He is CEO of Def Jam records and Roc-a-Fella records, which he founded with Damon "Dame" Dash and Kareem "Biggs" Burke.

From the beginning of his commercial recording career, Jay-Z chose a route that many would consider untraditional. When no major label gave him a record deal, Jay-Z created Roc-A-Fella Records as his own independent label. After striking a deal with Priority to distribute his material, Jay-Z released his 1996 debut album Reasonable Doubt, with beats from acclaimed producers such as DJ Premier and Clark Kent, and a notable appearance by The Notorious B.I.G. The album received critical acclaim and eventually obtained platinum status in the US.

If people who struggled with being born into poverty and overcoming the pressures of crime and drugs that such neighbourhoods too often promote as a way of earning a living can rise to lead lives of fame and fortune, then so can you. You have the benefit of seeing those who "made it" and following suggestions offered as a path to success. The road has already been paved. All one has to do now is travel down it with passion and purpose.

Jay-Z's music has crossed genre lines as well, and he has collaborated on projects with rock groups like Linkin Park. Gone are the days of "white music" and "black music." Because of artists like Jay-Z, there is a mutual sharing and respect of all music types throughout the industry.

Jay-Z also co-owns the New Jersey Nets NBA team and has several other entrepreneurial ventures. His love of music and artistic talent led to his success, but because he is able to be freely creative, he has some businesses and investments many would think of as "ultimate toys." One may aspire to be a famous athlete, but it is an even loftier goal to aspire to own the team.

Another inspiring entrepreneurial mogul of the rap recording industry shares a similar background and success story. Sean Combs, better known a P. Diddy, was born in the Harlem section of New York City, an area well-known for the drugs, crime and violence that has plagued its mostly poverty-stricken, ethnically diverse population. Sean's "street hustler" father was murdered at the age of just thirty three, when Sean was only two. In order to provide a better life for her two children, his mother Janice Combs moved her children to Mount Vernon, New York, and worked three jobs to assure them a quality education. Sean graduated from a Catholic boy's high school and headed off to Howard University in Washington, D.C., but dropped out to pursue an internship at Uptown Records, where he quickly became a successful executive.

At just nineteen years old, Combs had been promoted to become one of the label's top executives, managing such notable acts as Father MC, Mary J. Blige, and Heavy D & the Boyz. The very first record that Combs produced, Jodeci's Come & Talk to Me, sold two million copies and led to Combs' promotion to vice president.

In fact, he was so successful he was fired! He says of this experience, "I guess Andre didn't want two kings in the castle....I had obtained some success, some notoriety, and I didn't realize it wasn't my house." So, he built his own "house." He started Bad Boy Entertainment with help from Arista Records founder Clive Davis. Combs, or P. Diddy's, company signed on many of his former acts from Uptown Records, but like Jay-Z the list of artists he promotes is not limited to the rap genre. He pursued his own musical artistry with unusual collaborations with artists such as David Bowie and Britney Spears in an attempt to innovate and find a new sound.

This type of musical collaboration by the great moguls of rap has opened many doors to new art, new ways of thinking about music, and the way society sees rap and hip-hop music. The creative processes of these entrepreneurs have opened new doors for all who follow them. P. Diddy also has his own clothing line and other business ventures because his success in music allowed him to finance and promote them. Again, new ways of thinking, being, and working in today's world are available to all of us because of those who went before and found their passion, purpose, vision, and pursued their goals.

There is no denying that P. Diddy, Jay-Z, and others in the industry have faced their share of obstacles even after obtaining success. The widely publicised feud between East and West Coast rappers in the United States is an issue that might have ruined weaker or less focused business people, but everyone has their burdens. How one handles these trials is a key factor in achieving success. The ability to overcome such negative publicity, whether or not the rumors and accusations are true, is an attribute of a person in line with his or her purpose. With higher levels of success often comes larger challenges, temptations and trials.

IF

"If you can keep your head when all about you

Are losing theirs and blaming it on you,

If you can trust yourself when all men doubt you,

But make allowance for their doubting too;

If you can wait and not be tired by waiting,

Or being lied about, don't deal in lies,

Or being hated, don't give way to hating,

And yet don't look too good, nor talk too wise:

If you can dream – and not make dreams your master;

If you can think – and not make thoughts your aim;

If you can meet with Triumph and Disaster

And treat those two impostors just the same;

If you can bear to hear the truth you've spoken

Twisted by knaves to make a trap for fools,

Or watch the things you gave your life to, broken,

And stoop and build 'em up with worn-out tools:

If you can make one heap of all your winnings

And risk it on one turn of pitch-and-toss,

And lose, and start again at your beginnings

And never breathe a word about your loss;

If you can force your heart and nerve and sinew

To serve your turn long after they are gone,

And so hold on when there is nothing in you

Except the Will which says to them: 'Hold on!'

If you can talk with crowds and keep your virtue,

Or walk with Kings – nor lose the common touch,

if neither foes nor loving friends can hurt you,

If all men count with you, but none too much;

If you can fill the unforgiving minute

With sixty seconds' worth of distance run,

Yours is the Earth and everything that's in it,

And – which is more – you'll be a Man, my son!"

Rudyard Kipling

Chapter Three

It's Your Power!
Taking it Back and Keeping It

Chapter Three

It's Your Power!
Taking it Back and Keeping It

We all know and love people who cannot wait to arrive at functions to tell us their latest disabilities, experiences of injustice or some other story of how their life remains "stuck" and why they cannot move forward in life. They feed off our sympathies and sometimes resent the successes of others. Yet they keep coming, looking for validation that truly life has been unkind and unfair to them.

Who amongst us has not had challenges or setbacks? Even the most seemingly privileged individuals and families have their share of road blocks. In a commencement speech given at Stanford University in 2005, Steve Jobs, co-founder of Apple Computers and Pixar Animation, stated that he was fired from a company – McIntosh/ Apple Computers – that he helped create! Rather than see this as some grand scheme by his colleagues, he saw this occurrence as a rebirth. It allowed him to reexamine what it is he truly loves to do. By redirecting his focus, Jobs was able to create one of the most prolific motion picture companies, and one that produced the first fully computer-animated film, Toy Story, in history. Eventually, Jobs tells us, Apple bought Pixar and he is once again fully integrated within the company he founded, but on a much higher level.

CHANGING YOUR FOCUS

I magine what could have happened to Steve Jobs if he'd become completely resentful toward the Apple Corporation and set his mind to destroying those who harmed him? How different would his life be had he remained in a victim mentality? He may have destroyed a company that wronged him, but at the same time he would have limited his future options, which in effect, turned out to be much grander than he could have imagined. I was struck by his admission in his speech of how he was fully to blame for his termination from Apple Computers.

So, one may wonder, is it good to be a failure? I'm not really saying that it is. What I'm reiterating, as I stated in chapter one, is that one should see "failures" as learning experiences and redirections, but not hang on to them whilst playing a sort of "blame game" or "culture of blame" by insulting others and, in the process, bringing down those around us to whom one inflicts these stories of woe.

One should see "failures" as learning experiences and redirections.

Perhaps you are guilty of complaining about a given situation. Then, something even more sorry manifests and you say, "What a coincidence! I've been fearing that ever since I bought this new Jaguar three months ago that I'd crash it," and wham, another vehicle rams you from behind. You didn't cause the crash, did you? It is surely a coincidence, right? Well, not in my opinion. When we focus on things with passion, we create them. Actually, we tend to create anything we focus on intently. Yes, you read that correctly. We create, manifest, and bring into being, all of our experiences. It is called the Law of Attraction (LOA). (Please refer to 'RAS' in chapter four if you are unfamiliar with LOA, or The Seven Universal laws in chapter seven) Author Lisa Nichols states, quite simply, "What we think about, we bring about." She further explains in the DVD The Secret that when we complain, we bring about more things to complain about! When we focus on things that make us joyful, we create those as well! So we need to pursue thoughts and actions that make us feel good! Put another way by entrepreneur Mike Dooley, "Thoughts become things." Why wouldn't we "choose the good ones?"

I think a chronically negative state of mind becomes a habit by those who complain and continue to complain, and they therefore foster anger and resentment. It is like a fungus or parasite that attaches itself to a host. It is literally so ingrained in these individuals to have a beef with someone or something that they see life as dark and out of their control. This is not to say that the most positive-thinking individuals don't have down days. They do, but the most successful people have made it a habit to see things in an optimistic fashion. Truly successful people recognise obstacles, but rather than allowing the obstruction in the path stop their progress, they become focused on the outcome of the situation. They see the end result and figure a way to get over or around the blockage. They move on. They focus their attention on the brightness of the future rather than the darkness of the past. If we follow Nichols' teachings, focusing on the failures, obstacles, injustices, heartbreaks, heartaches, scarcity, lack, etc. of our past, then we create more of that. I say we learn to practice focusing on the beauty and abundance of the future – to forgive the past and let it go.

Now this brings to mind another issue. If we are to forgive the past and learn from it, and at the same time I'm saying to you that we created our past by what we thought about, then to whom do we owe forgiveness? We start with ourselves! Forgiving others will come more easily for us when we can first forgive ourselves for our humanness.

NAME
NOM

No.

We created our past by what we thought about, then to whom do we owe forgiveness?

Let's take the example of abused women who repeatedly choose men or relationships that are also abusive. According to the Law of Attraction, we created or attracted the abusive relationship. Let me stop here and say that I do not excuse any abuser. It is also good to note here that we cannot control the thoughts and actions of another human being. We can influence them, but it is only a positive experience when we are in a state of overflowing self-confidence. When our self-image is good, we attract and can influence others to become better. We cannot make someone else into something or someone else. A person's behaviour and attitude is their own, but what is our participation in a given relationship?

We all know someone in a "bad" relationship and we bemoan our friend or family member's situation wondering, "Why does she/ he stay with him/ her?" But how do we know of the situation in the first place? We know because one of them complains. We hear them verbalise the horrid situation they are in. We feel compassion, and we want to help her flee, yet she stays. Or he stays. They then continue to complain, and things escalate in a way that is heart-wrenching.

A BIT MORE ABOUT ME

Growing up, I always reminded myself that "what the mind can conceive and believe, it can achieve." Looking back now, I cannot remember where I first heard this, but it was a phrase I never forgot or stopped believing in. Only years later did I come to realise that those were the inspiring words of the late, great Napoleon Hill, author of the bestselling book Think and Grow Rich, amongst others.

From the age of fifteen, when I ended up in the care of the local authority, to present day, I have witnessed and experienced many situations which I chose to use as a turning point for growth. I always believed that I should be with my grandparents, and after three months of interviews with social workers, that was indeed where I was placed. In my mind, I always had the ability to get what I wanted, though there was a time when I didn't always use this in the most positive of ways.

For many years I was plagued with anger and resentment, but another phrase which always kept me focused during that period was "success is the best revenge." Not that I ever wanted revenge, as I see this mentality as one that holds us back, but I always pitied those who wronged me even though it still hurt immensely, and I felt I could prove my worth to them by succeeding. Then they'd see that they were the one in the wrong. I've since come to realise that anger is what I'd seek out and choose to ignite in others! The one whose approval I really needed was my own!

CHANGING OUR RESPONSES TO NEGATIVITY

Having very low EQ, or "emotional intelligence," and maybe being slightly manipulative, I would hone in on the weaknesses of others and then wonder why they were provoked by what I had said or done. I was in a place where I was addicted to negative emotions, which kept me playing the part of the victim. Remember, all thoughts are emotionally based, and I could not stop dwelling on negatives of the past, which were in turn preventing my emotional growth. This cycle includes attracting people and situations which will confirm these emotions, thus keeping one addicted.

We spoke about the power of the subconscious mind in chapter one and this is exactly where these kinds of thoughts lie. Nobody would consciously choose to keep themselves in pain. We move towards pleasure in order to avoid pain, but when the pain we are experiencing is tied into our emotional addiction of repeating destructive events, our subconscious mind cannot reject this habitual behaviour. When, however, you become consciously aware that this is indeed what is taking place, the behaviour dissipates. In The Power of Now, Eckhart Tolle explains the dissipation of this destructive cycle as meaning "that it cannot use you anymore by pretending to be you, and it can no longer replenish itself through you. You have found your own innermost strength."

EMOTIONAL CONTAGION

By being in the company of individuals who are experiencing such a cycle, we can become the receiver of emotional contagion. One can become empathetic of positive or negative emotions, but when we are in the presence of those who continually display destructive emotions, and we mirror this behaviour, we find ourselves in a "tit for tat" situation with no one taking responsibility for their actions. In other words, it is a "blame culture." We become so rehearsed and comfortable in this blame culture that we are drawn down, in the words of Dr. Ginger Bowler, "below the line." Dr. Bowler, in her book, Listening and Communicating with Energy, presents an "energy model for understanding our energies and how to manage negative and positive behaviours, and negative and positive emotions." Her model and 16 rules can be found in the back of this book on page 187. Simply put, there are behaviours, thoughts and emotions which are within our integrity. This is a concept even small children can understand. They understand right from wrong, but sometimes, as with adults, children must learn from trial and error.

The pain we are experiencing is tied into our emotional addiction of repeating destructive events.

When we operate within this integrity, or what is right for us, then "life works." Dr. Bowler refers to this as "operating above the line." When, however, we continually operate in ways that are contradictory to what is within our systems of integrity, ethics, and morals, we are then operating below the line. This is not to say that one negative thought, action or emotion drags one into a life of negativity or operating within the blame culture, but one who operates chronically in this fashion will find that they continually create more of the drama, upset and chaos about which they complain. The tit for tat tennis match of the blame culture is a consistent part of one's life and can be difficult to let go of because one becomes so accustomed to it!

The transfer of emotional contagion can happen for good or bad in any type of relationship. It takes place in groups, teams and societies, but in the event of these being negative emotions, only the awareness of one's own actions, learning new responses, and even removing oneself from the situation can solve this. This is another area which can be beautifully handled by psychometrics. The process of the personality measure and recognizing where on the chart we live in our mind can help us identify areas that can be changed or improved upon. So, though we recognize the negativity one may bring into any relationship, the way to remedy this is to focus on the positive, thereby replacing the old habit of blame with new positive thoughts, actions, emotions, and feelings.

OUR FUNCTION WITHIN A TEAM

Team dynamics is about each individual understanding themselves whilst understanding the differences they have from other team members and valuing those differences. A great team is made up of people who understand their individual power whilst complimenting one another, not by mirroring each other. Synergy is created through individuals being influenced into playing his or her role well, and allowing other team members to do the same. If this doesn't happen and a blame culture emerges, a ripple effect can take place creating a collective emotion. For example, in a sales situation an enthused emotion is one we set out to create. However, what might the emotions be of a salesperson who has not made the last ten sales? That would depend on what their thoughts are. If the thoughts were of not getting the sale, they may unwittingly transmit those thoughts through their emotions to the prospective or established client. How would that translate to the rest of the sales team if that salesperson is considered to be the best in that organisation? Though sales positions are competitive by nature, buying into the negative emotions of one seen as "the best" salesperson can set in motion a low income day for those around him or her.

It is a common question for a salesperson to enter his or her place of business and ask others, "How is business today?" If the response is "Slow," one may move more slowly, thereby creating a slower pace, but if the response is, "It's busy! We're rocking and rolling! I've closed four deals already and it isn't even noon!" then one becomes enthused and "on one's toes." If indeed "like attracts like," as the Law of Attraction states, then activity creates activity. In sales, more prospects means more possible sales.

Think about walking through a shopping centre or any retail establishment. If the atmosphere is upbeat and joyful, one may find oneself drawn into the store. If one is in a negative state of mind, one may want to "not be bothered with the crowd." The very idea of "big sales events" with discounted merchandise is a marketing idea to draw in customers. Activity begets activity, producing sales, which is the bottom line. So indeed we need to maintain positive thoughts in order for positive emotional contagion to exist.

There are times, however, when detachment is the only way to maintain our own harmonious balance. Real detachment means fostering inner strength and an ability to function calmly with full inner control in all circumstances. A detached person is not harassed or hurried, and can do everything with concentration and attention, whether the situation is too many customers to handle efficiently or the lack of walk-in customers, as a retail sales example. This ensures a successful outcome to his or her actions though it seems to indicate that one is not fully attached to the specifics of the outcome. One client on a slow day has the potential to spend more than several others combined, especially if the attitude of the salesperson is one of detachment. By this I mean that if the salesperson is focused on serving the needs or desires of the client or customer, they might just spend more time and money because they are not only buying a product, but they are buying, in many instances, the services of the salesperson, such as product knowledge. People want to be around others who are "above the line." Like attracts like. The blame culture promotes upset, chaos, and ill-tempered individuals. Stated so simply, which one would you really prefer to choose each day? It really can be that simple, once we practice what we know.

We need to take responsibility for our own actions, and realise that controlling another person into doing what we want them to do will not make us happy. Relationships are not about us allowing another person to bring us happiness; relationships are about us growing to the point where we are happy, regardless. If our happiness is dependant on another person's approval, we are not the owner of our happiness. If we expect someone to follow a set of given rules and guidelines in order to make us happy, then we are not allowing them free will and are little more than dictators. Our happiness is our own, and when this falls in line with another person's we can create true harmony, but this should never be at the expense of another person's happiness. We live up to our own expectations, and unless stated, a partner cannot know our every need. It's too easy to say, "I would have expected more from you," but sometimes we have expectations without stating clearly what we truly desire. We may even ask ourselves at times why a certain person is behaving in this manner or why they are doing this "to me," when understanding that truly happy people do not do or say things to make others unhappy. The Dalai Lama once said that if someone gives you a gift and you don't accept it, who does the gift then belong to? Remembering this allows us not to accept negative emotions from others as our own.

CHANGING OUR RESPONSES

There are many ways we can begin to initiate change in our lives. First of all, we can recognise our strengths and weaknesses, and commit to bettering our lives by changing our responses.

It isn't always easy. The first step is to stop reacting. What I mean by this is that when we are faced with an issue or emotion, we frequently react without thinking. Let's say someone cuts us up in traffic. Do we immediately react with anger and choice words insulting the driving abilities of the offending driver, and possibly also displaying a negative gesture indicating our displeasure? It is a common reaction, but what does it do for us? The momentary perceived negative action then puts us in a state of anger and frustration, so we react with more negativity, initiating the tit for tat cycle of the blame culture.

That car is going to drive off. They're no longer affected by our negative response, one hopes. Yet often, we let this scenario continue to wreak havoc on our day. We share the episode with the next lot of people we come in contact with. We perpetuate the cycle. We share the story, we express how much it rattled us, and then we draw to us more of this negativity. A co-worker may respond with a story of being jostled by the crowd on the Underground or bus, and someone else may share their experience about being caused some injustice at home. The day proceeds in a state of negativity and possible chaos. No one smiles. The photocopier, which may not have worked properly before, is suddenly a beast that everyone hates. Clients, the very lifeblood of the business, are seen as and treated like nuisances versus being valued as the most important factor of business life. They can and do pick up on this, thereby affecting the business' bottom line, and even worse, anyone and everyone affected by the negativity may bring the sour mood home to their unsuspecting and most likely undeserving families.

So what if instead of responding to the traffic maneuver with negativity, we smile, let it go, and think, "Whoops! What a blessing that a possible mishap has been avoided and we're all still going about our day. And what a lovely day it is!" This can be done during inclement weather, too. Lighting storms and rain are part of nature's agenda; the Earth needs it. So, if we rewind the scenario, and one is cut up in traffic, smiles and lets the offense go, and then still repeats the story to co-workers with a smile of relief as we share, "I had a near miss in traffic this morning. I'm so glad I was able to avoid an accident," then the shared stories will likely be those of equal gratitude of arriving to work safely. That photocopying machine may indeed still not work, but the inanimate object, because of the attitude of those using it, will simply be "a hardworking machine that has served us well." The paper-jams and misfeeds are dealt with without much complaint. Don't we all know people who pat their computer monitors lovingly thinking that if they treat their PC with kindness it will work better for them? That seemingly silly gesture keeps the computer user in a positive mindset, allowing him or her to figure out what is holding up the technology.

So that is a simple first step that can be applied to all relationships. In interpersonal relationships, we can simply not respond to offensive words and actions with negativity. That can be very difficult when someone you love hurts you. For instance, when dealing with children we are much more likely to respond without anger to an accident; however, if we think the child knew better than to dump a bucket of water onto the kitchen floor in order to make a lake to float his boat on, then we may respond with a bit of anger. Then the child cries, the cries upset the caretaker, who is already in a state of frustration, and the cleaning up process is one of hostility.

If, however we don't respond in anger, and we let the child know we are not impressed by this action, however creative it was, and that he must help in the cleaning up process, then perhaps a better body of water can be created to facilitate the youngster's desire to float his boat. Again, this can be difficult to practice, especially if one has dinner guests coming shortly. The way we repeat the story to friends, either an endearing action of a small child versus how much it angered you, will totally change or create the atmosphere of the evening. Children do often learn by trial and error. We all do.

It can be difficult to handle responses that have been part of our personality for many years. There are many, many ways to help us retain our peace in a situation of offense. Yoga as a form of exercise and meditation is great. Some participants claim it has been around for six thousand years. Actually, any type of meditation that suits you is good. What I mean by meditation is sitting or posing quietly with the intention of quieting the mind. There is an old saying that "prayer is when we petition God for something. Meditation is when we listen for the response."

Quieting our mind causes us to still our bodies, and therefore it helps us practice being in a state of tranquility and more effectively gaining control of our emotional responses. One of my favorite methods for quieting and reflecting on myself is called "floating." This is done in spas, and the participant floats in eight to ten inches of water saturated with Epsom salts for an hour. The body floats weightlessly. It literally takes "the weight of the world" (figuratively and literally) off of the participant. The London Float Centre says this about the effects of their services:

"Floating" is a wonderful way of attaining the deepest relaxation – it has been said that just one hour of floating can have the effect of four hours of deep sleep.

In the gravity free environment the body balances and heals internally as all the senses are rested. Research shows that floating measurably reduces blood pressure and heart rate whilst lowering the levels of stress related chemicals in the body.

Flotation therapy is used widely in the treatment of stress, anxiety, jet lag and to improve concentration and creativity. Sports performance and 'wind-down' is also enhanced during floating. Also, one hour of floating has the restorative effects of four hours of sleep!

During a float, you produce slower brain-waves patterns, known as theta waves, which are normally experienced only during a deep meditation or just before falling asleep and when waking up. This is usually accompanied by vivid imagery, very clear, creative thoughts, sudden insights and inspirations or feelings of profound peace and joy, induced by the release of endorphins, the body's natural opiates. Because of these effects, floating is used effectively in the treatment of depression and addictions, including smoking and alcohol. It is also used in schools and universities as a tool for Super Learning.

> Quieting our mind causes us to still our bodies, and therefore it helps us practice being in a state of tranquility.

Depending on your own journey through life, a float might provide an hour of total physical relaxation – or a profound healing experience, emotionally and spiritually transforming. Floating can be a wonderful aid to opening doors into your inner world, gradually allowing access to those deeper levels at which real changes take place."

www.londonfloatcentre.com

This type of meditation and detoxification practice is wonderful at uniting the health of the mind, or self-image, with the health of the body. When one is out of balance, the other is as well. We cannot neglect our physical bodies in pursuit of the perfect mind. In fact, the entire basis for the teachings of Siddhartha Gautama, who lived in the Himalayas in the sixth century BC, and is more commonly known as "The Buddha," is that we must follow "the Middle Path" to enlightenment. The Buddha says, "Nothing in excess." We cannot starve or overfeed the body because it will interfere with our ability to meditate. You cannot be in a quiet state if you are starving, and overeating tends to make us lethargic. Floating, in my opinion, helps us deal with both the physical trials our body is facing while at the same time allowing us time to meditate and reflect on whatever our emotional needs are at that time. It is a way to truly take care of our entire "self."

Since we all know that our food and beverage choices affect our bodies and our minds, careful selection should be practiced. Luckily, there are detoxification practices such as floating, colonic irrigation, diets, fasts and supplements to counteract bad choices. As stated earlier in this chapter, choosing the wrong foods, or a "below the line action" will not draw you into negativity, but too frequently choosing the wrong foods may. There are nutritional requirements for our bodies to operate ideally. Too many processed foods, for example, may satisfy us initially, but they give us very little of the nutrients we need to function in a state of health and mental clarity.

Carrying too much or too little weight, abusing street or pharmaceutical drugs, smoking, drinking, etc., in excess robs us of our power as well as the nutrients our bodies need. When we don't feel well, we cannot function in a proper emotional state. It is nearly impossible to be calm and controlled in your emotional responses with a hangover and a severe case of indigestion.

The issue of diet is so personal. For many years, I had extremely poor eating habits which probably led to me now having an underactive thyroid gland, which no one else in my family has. Eating habits can also be cultural. It is difficult to let go of the "bad" cooking habits of one's homeland, culture or familial practices, and this need not be. There are hundreds of great diets and ways of eating. In fact, the basis for the hit diet book Eat Right for Your Type uses your blood type and determines what foods work best in your chemical make-up. It takes diet back through history to the foods that probably ended up being your cultural favorites anyway. Though that book is only one of many, it may be necessary to find the right eating style for you, which may change as you age. Also, certain health issues may require abstention from certain foods or ways of preparing foods. Before starting any diet, it is always a good idea to consult your physician to see what your needs are.

Exercise is also important, and it should be fun. Do what brings you joy. Get up and move daily. One of my favorite exercise activities is dancing to hip-hop. Not only does it provide me with an outlet for exercise, it also provide my sons with the entertainment of laughing at Mum trying to do the latest dance moves, and it elevates my mood. It is mood-enhancing. This chapter is designed to show you that you need not remain a victim of the blame culture because when we are in a state of joy, we cannot also be a victim. Philosopher Bob Proctor says that disease is the body not being at ease. "Disease cannot exist in a body that is at ease." In other words, in order for your body to operate optimally, you must be at peace with yourself.

Reclaiming power over our lives means we start with reclaiming the power we have over our body and mind. Then we choose more appropriate responses to the negative situations and emotions we face. We cannot change another person, but we can control our own emotions. This is how we begin to reclaim our power and keep it. We must be true to ourselves. We first need to work out who we are, and this can be easily done with self-reflective practices such as psychometrics, meditation, diet and exercise. It is just one of those "truths" in life. We must first care for ourselves and enjoy ourselves before anyone else can care for us and enjoy our company.

THE GREATEST LOVE OF ALL

"I decided long ago, never to walk in anyone's shadows

If I fail, if I succeed

At least I'll live as I believe

No matter what they take from me

They can't take away my dignity

Because the greatest love of all

Is happening to me

I found the greatest love of all

Inside of me

The greatest love of all

Is easy to achieve

Learning to love yourself

It is the greatest love of all"

(words and music by

Michael Masser and Linda Creed)

Chapter Four

Coincidence? I Think Not!

Chapter Four

Coincidence? I Think Not!

A ll of my favourite films and television programmes have the same running vein: science fiction. Not in the Star Trek /outer space sense, but the ones which I can really get lost in because they could almost be "real" - films like Back to the Future and Sliding Doors, and television hits such as Quantum Leap or even Beyond Belief: Fact or Fiction to name but a few. These films and programmes always made me feel as though there was some kind of message I was to decipher, whilst Forrest Gump reinforced my belief that anything is possible no matter who you are. My belief that the truth is stranger than fiction has allowed amazing events to take place in my life that many people simply would have put down to coincidence.

From a very early age, I would listen religiously to the Top 40 pop chart rundown on a Sunday afternoon with my aunt, who was an avid popular music fan. I would make the routine of listening passively a little more interesting by predicting who I thought would be in the number one position each week. After many years of doing this, I developed what Malcolm Gladwell would call the "blink" ability to be able to successfully predict which new releases would become hits and which ones wouldn't make it into the top ten. At such an early age, this was simply fun, and I had no idea how useful this would be to me in the future. These positive "mind games" actually work on other areas of our life because of how we become accustomed to thinking.

My love for music never waned, and new technology allowed non-musically trained types such as me to make professional sounding music without having to know how to play any musical instruments. Whilst on a Business & Technology Education Council (BTEC) national diploma course at South Thames College in London studying popular music, I became very good friends with many talented people. There were two friends in particular with whom I made a habit of writing and performing songs for our end-of-term exams. The very last song I ever wrote during my time at the college later went on to become a number four hit in the British national charts. How? Well, I would make it a rule to copyright every song or even verse I wrote. For some reason, I would follow this act by saying, "I copyright all of my material so that I can make loads of money when someone nicks one of my songs." This became a running joke and friends would snigger at my level of caution. This was, however, exactly how I became the co-writer of a hit track! My friend from college told me that whilst in the recording booth at a studio, the first song which came to her mind was one which I had written. The song was an underground smash for over a year before it hit the charts, and during this same period I gained everything I'd always intended to achieve in this area; I was signed in a completely separate deal to Virgin Records. This is just a coincidence you may say, but when you understand what I referred to in the previous chapter as the Law of Attraction, you understand that the thoughts which you hold to be true in your mind will manifest.

UNDERSTANDING THE PRACTICE OF SUCCESSFUL THINKING

There is a simple exercise which motivational giant Tony Robbins uses to explain how we focus on what we are looking for. He asks you to look around the room for everything that is green and then close your eyes. Now name everything that is brown. You were not looking for brown so unless you know the room you are in very well, it will be near impossible for you to name any brown objects in that room. In a sense, you can only recall and thereby manifest those things toward which you directed your attention and intention.

Many would say that I was lucky that my friend had recorded my song in order to make it a hit. Indeed I was, but to use another Tony Robbins quote, "Luck is when preparation meets opportunity." Opportunity dances with those already on the dance floor, and I had been prepared for a very long time. In Life's a Pitch, Stephen Bayley and Roger Mavity state that, "life may be lived forwards, but only explained backwards." We cannot always see how things connect until we look back and, in the words of Steve Jobs, "connect the dots."

So, you've become a pro at getting tables in the best restaurants by intending that they exist.

Another way to put this exercise in practice is to think about going to your favorite restaurant on a Friday night. It will very likely be crowded and, if you don't have a reservation, you may have to wait for quite some time. Instead of giving up because you think there is no way you'll get a table, try thinking that you'll get right in. Maybe you have the thought to call ahead, but you know you'll miss the reservation deadline. Intend that there is a space for you. Actually "know" that a table you want (no need to create one next to the kitchen if this really disturbs you) when you want it will be available. It will take some practice, but you'll find that this simple step to developing this positive habit will grow. You'll learn to manipulate it to fit your needs and wants.

So, you've become a pro at getting tables in the best restaurants by intending that they exist. What next? Apply this thought habit to finding parking spaces, getting phone calls and emails, and then move it up a notch for whatever it is you find you want. Maybe you want a new car. Maybe you want a client to pay who has not kept their agreement financially. Maybe you need or want three new clients today. Intend them.

It should be quite clear by now that indeed, the mind is the key to success. The previous chapters have all addressed the positive and negative things that can and do occur depending on the thinker's state of mind, attitude, habits and knowledge of the self. Now how do we harness this power?

Many of history's great thinkers have had profound sayings regarding the power of the mind. I've already mentioned Napoleon Hill's statement, "What a man can conceive he can achieve," Mike Dooley's "Thoughts become things," and Lisa Nichols' "What we think about, we bring about." It is clear, too, from chapter three that the mind can be instrumental in bringing about negative thoughts and ideas.

It takes a good bit of practice for many people to remember the Law of Attraction. Often we've become so used to wallowing in "stinking thinking." I like to look at the outcomes of certain situations and see what my part in it was. I enjoy maintaining an expectant attitude and the "chance encounters" of running into old friends, finding a lost item I'd set my mind to retrieving and other situations, but it is also handy for us to look at those situations that did not turn out as intended. Were they hindered by fear? Did we buy into someone else's negativity? Did we create the negativity on our own? Or what if it just didn't serve us well? Or did they?

I have a friend who recently began a project with someone who quickly not only killed the project out of the blue, but then tried to destroy her professionally. The point of me mentioning this is that sometimes we attract situations to learn something about ourselves, and when we really get the lesson we created for ourselves, then we grow, like Steve Jobs, into a position that is much grander. When we allow the negativity, especially that of someone else to affect us internally, we shrink, we diminish, and we sink "below the line." Retaliation and revenge is a below the line action whether it is in a professional or personal situation. How differently might the outcome of my friend recording my lyrics have been had I reacted negatively to her using them without first obtaining my permission? It is no coincidence that we have the experiences in life that we do. Recognizing opportunities for growth is another factor in moving into a realm of personal success in all areas of life.

APPLYING OUR THINKING TO INTER-PERSONAL RELATIONSHIPS

Remember relationships - I mean intimate relationships? Ever look back at one that ended painfully and say, "I learned a lot!" Do you mean it? Many romantic relationships end so painfully that the individuals have nothing but bitterness and resentment toward each other, but real growth occurs when we can look back at these situations and thank these people for the growth they allowed us to experience. They were attracted into our lives by us. We experienced something with them. Did we grow, or did it hold us back? Do we continue to verbalise the horridness of the situation? If you answer "yes" to this last statement, have you created subsequent relationships that are much the same? Or what if a partner cheated on you with another person? Did you then create a relationship of retaliation and then you cheated? And then what? Did you grow?

There are no coincidences. We create our realities because of our thoughts. We create our own happiness. When we look at our past and suffer again and again over prior injustices, then we continue to create similar injustices that keep us stuck. Yet if we forgive, and we come to a place of true forgiveness and gratitude for the lessons learned, it can be liberating and life-altering. We've all heard the saying, "It took everything you've been through to make you who you are today." Most of us accept that on the surface. It is easier to do if we like ourselves. It is even easier if we truly adore ourselves, but it isn't often that we run into people who adore themselves without bridging over into some annoying form of narcissism. This is not what I mean. What I am referring to are people who enjoy their own company. Do you know people who can be happy in most situations? Don't you just love to be around them? They seem comfortable in almost any situation. Being around them often just elevates our mood.

Don't we all know people who can't be happy for any reason? I'm not insinuating that issues of grief, such as the loss of a loved one whether to death, divorce or other real life situation, is not appropriate. Grief is different from chronic depression. Grief is an emotion that is really important to address in the moment. We don't process the situation if we don't grieve effectively.

However, many people who are medicated for "depression," in my opinion, have simply practiced a way of being unhappy. When they resort too quickly to medication, which is often not the intention of physicians to be a long-term solution, then they are frequently incapable, because of the medication, of looking at their minds and how to remedy what they've created. It is no coincidence that we have a more depressed society since the development of new and "better" anti-depressants, some of which, ironically, have warnings for creating suicidal tendencies!

That paragraph may really rub you the wrong way, especially if you are currently medicated for depression, but you picked up this book in order to find a way to better your life, didn't you? Never quit taking medication without first discussing it with a medical professional, but if you are prescribed mood-altering substances, have you addressed, effectively, the issues for which you were initially diagnosed as needing these drugs for? It is no coincidence that when we look for ways to improve, they are often presented to us. Sometimes they are in ways that we do not want to hear because we have habits which we don't want to break.

Have you ever heard someone leave a doctor's office say, "Good news! All I have to do is quit smoking and drinking excessively and totally change my diet, and then I'll be in perfect health?" Who would argue that any of those things are good for you? They're all bad habits which can be replaced by good habits, but sometimes humans just don't want to let go of their identifying habits.

It is no coincidence that people who smoke die from lung cancer more frequently than those who don't. Heavy drinkers have their own set of health problems. Overeaters do too, as well as those who don't eat much at all. We can easily see how we create our physical health. I say the same goes for emotional and some mental health as well. We create it; now we must find, if it is appropriate, how to remedy what we've created. Your good health, be it physical, emotional, mental, or financial is all in your hands - or should I say, in your mind.

RAS – NO, NOT AS IN RASTAFARIAN!

Another way to explain the Law of Attraction, and indeed how goal-setting works, is to understand how our Reticular Activity System (RAS) works. This is the part of our brain which filters information in order to highlight whatever you've told it to look out for. So for instance, you could learn a new word then suddenly notice that day everyone is using that word, whereas before your attention was brought to the existence of this word, you hadn't noticed it being used. Scientific research has established the fact that the RAS, a group of cells at the base of your brain stem (about the size of a little finger) serves as a little control centre sorting and evaluating incoming information. It's responsible for filtering out the urgent stuff from the unimportant so that you can function properly.

Dr. Henriette Anne Klauser, author of the bestselling books *Writing on Both Sides of the Brain, Put Your Heart on Paper,* and her most recent book, *Write it Down, Make it Happen* has this to say about the power of the mind and a physiological truth that occurs within us:

"At the base of the brain stem, about the size of a little finger, is a group of cells whose job it is to sort and evaluate incoming data. This control center is known as the Reticular Activating System (RAS). The RAS sends the urgent stuff to the active part of your brain, and sends the non-urgent to the subconscious. The RAS awakens the brain to consciousness, and keeps it alert – just as surely as your baby's cry in the night, from all the way down the hall, can waken you from a deep sleep. The RAS evaluates the nonessential nighttime noises – the dripping faucet, the crickets, or neighborhood traffic – and filters out the non-urgent, waking you up only for the urgent. The baby cries, and in a split second you are bolt upright in bed, wide awake and ready to rescue the infant in distress.

The keenest, most familiar example of the Reticular Activating System at work is an experience all of us have had at one time or another. You are in a packed room; you can barely hear the conversation of the person you are talking to above the din of the crowd. Suddenly, someone clear on the other side of the room mentions your name. And that one word cuts through the sea of sound and your ears immediately perk up. You turn your head toward the speaker, eager now to tune in the rest of what he or she is saying about you, straining to hear if it is good news, ready to defend the bad....

Although you may think you are giving your conversational companion undivided attention, the fact is your attention is fragmented and subconsciously taking in the Tower of Babel around you, sorting, sorting, sorting, even as you speak. Your name when spoken stands out as prominently as a speck of gold in a miner's pan of gravel.

The RAS is like a filtering system of the brain. Writing it down sets up the filter. Things start to appear – it's a matter of your filtering system.

If you have never owned a Honda before, and you buy a blue Honda, all of a sudden you see blue Hondas all over town. You might wonder, 'Where are all these blue Hondas coming from?' But they were there all along; you were just not paying attention to them.

Although you may think you are giving your conversational companion undivided attention, the fact is your attention is fragmented and subconsciously taking in the Tower of Babel around you, sorting, sorting, sorting, even as you speak.

Putting a goal in writing is like buying a blue Honda; it sets up a filter that helps you be aware of certain things in your surroundings. Writing triggers the RAS, which in turn sends a signal to the cerebral cortex: "Wake up! Pay attention! Don't miss this detail!" Once you write down a goal, your brain will be working overtime to see you get it, and will alert you to the signs and signals that, like the blue Honda, were there all along."

Mark Batterson, author of In a Pit with a Lion on a Snowy Day and ID: The True You, further explains this phenomenon:

"The Reticular Activating System (RAS) is **a cluster of nerve cells** in the brainstem that regulate alertness and attention. We are bombarded by thousands of stimuli every second – different sights, sounds and sensations. It is the job of the RAS to **regulate which stimuli you pay attention to and which stimuli you ignore**. It is the gatekeeper or **screening device**. Or think of it as **mental radar**. The RAS determines what you notice and what goes unnoticed.

Here's how it works. When you purchase a cell phone or clothing or a car, **it creates a category in your reticular activating system**. You notice if someone's cell phone has the same ringtone don't you? Because you go to answer yours! You notice if someone is wearing your outfit at the same event. Can you say awkward? And the second you drive your new car out of the lot, it seems like everyone is driving your model car.

That is the function of the RAS. You didn't have a category for your clothing or ringtone or car before you bought it. But once you made the purchase or downloaded the ringtone or drove out of the dealership, you had **a new cognitive category**.

SO WHAT DOES THAT HAVE TO DO WITH GOALS?

G oals create cognitive categories. And you begin to notice anything and everything that will help you achieve that goal."

You might have heard of Jim Carrey's RAS activating trick. When Carrey was just a stand-up comic in Los Angeles (before the movies and even before In Living Color), he decided he was going to write a cheque to himself for $12,000,000 for future services rendered. He carried that cheque in his wallet for years whilst working his way through the stand-up acts to TV until he finally got his cheque for his first movie, Ace Ventura. How much was that cheque for? $12,000,000.

The next time you're in the Planet Hollywood in New York City, take a look at the letter hanging on the wall that Bruce Lee wrote to himself. It's stamped "secret" and is dated January 9, 1970. What was Bruce's goal? "By 1980, I will be the best known oriental movie star in the United States and will have secured $10 million dollars." He continues with, "And in return I will give the very best acting I could possibly give every single time I am in front of the camera, and I will live in peace and harmony." Maybe this was just a coincidence also, but if we learn to use our RAS to bring to our attention people, things and situations which will take us closer to our desires, as long as we're not harming anyone, who cares if it seems ever so slightly coincidental? Obviously, it takes a lot more than simply writing a goal down or pinning a picture on a vision board to make it happen, but the act of committing your goals to paper not only starts the conscious process, it enables your mind to start working for you on other levels as well.

Scientific evidence of the brain and its functions support the idea that what we think about we bring about, and the act of writing out our goals further supports the process. It takes the idea of our thoughts creating our reality to a new level. When we put our thoughts, visions and goals on paper, it helps them to manifest quicker because we've created a new place for them. We can define them. We know what they look like. My habit of writing and copyrighting my song lyrics, and stating that I intended them to be hits, created my success. It was a habit I had envisioned, written down, and stated.

We can practice this yet further by including other senses in the process. If in fact, you are in the market for a new car, or if it is simply one of your goals, having a photograph or manufacturer's advertisement of the exact car you'd like to own on your goal card or vision board will more precisely define what it is you want to attract. Another tactic would be to visit a car dealership and sit in the car. Feel the seats, smell the scent of a new car, and feel the steering wheel in your hands. Take it for a test drive and mentally record, (and later write it down) what it feels like to drive it. Adding these sensory perceptions to your RAS will heighten the awareness of the vehicle and speed up the processes.

ENVISIONING RELATIONSHIPS?

This brings to mind trying to envision a relationship. Here, the example is not quite so applicable since one may not arrive at a good conclusion by "test driving" relationships not yet established, or posting pictures of the ideal beloved on a vision board. One may get to a place of stalking or trying to control another, which is not a good thing to do. Yet there are practices to put into action nonetheless. Envision what love feels like. Watch romantic movies and try to imagine yourself in place of the actors, and feel the love, but, it may be a good idea to lose the attachment to the physical appearance for the time being. Be open to love. Be willing to see that it may very well be around you at the very moment, but if it is not, you cannot force it into being. By being at peace with yourself and experiencing true inner joy, you will attract others who love you.

Love comes in many forms. When we are grateful for the love of a child, pets, a parent or grandparent, friends, etc., we are then in a state of emotional abundance; then romantic love comes. Think about it. Are you attracted to downtrodden people crying in their beers, or do most people gravitate toward those who are smiling, laughing, dancing and otherwise in a state of joy to just being themselves? So whom then do you think will be attracted to you? In what state are you at your most beautiful?

"When you live your life with an appreciation of coincidences and their meanings, you connect with the underlying field of infinite possibilities."

Deepak Chopra

"If you do something once, people will call it an accident.
If you do it twice, they call it a coincidence. But do it a third time and you've just proven a natural law."

Grace Murray Hopper

"Coincidence is God's way of remaining anonymous."

Albert Einstein

"Motivating gets you going and habit gets you there. Make motivating a habit and you will get there more quickly and have more fun on the trip."

Zig Ziglar

"Desire is the key to motivation, but it's the determination and commitment to an unrelenting pursuit of your goal – a commitment to excellence – that will enable you to attain the success you seek."

Mario Andretti - race car driver

Chapter Five

Moving Forward
Now That You Understand
Where You've Been

Chapter Five

Moving Forward Now That You Understand Where You've Been

M oving on can be tough. Many milestones in life are met with mixed emotions. Weddings and leaving school are often tearful events, though one is on the brink of an exciting new life. It can be hard to see the future with eager anticipation if one is afraid of what is coming. People sometimes dread the future because they fear change, but change is inevitable.

In the realm of physics, we know that no particles in the universe are ever stationary. Everything is constantly in flux, and human beings, with their human emotions and situations, are no different. Being able to ride the waves of the storm is a valuable skill if one is to enjoy boating, too.

Though it was a blessing to finally be signed to a major record label, a dream I had held for as long as I can remember, the challenges I faced as an artist from that point on were far from what I ever expected. I'd learnt at college how many hit songs reflected what took place sociologically, but at no time did anyone ever mention that sociological effects could cause radio stations not to play a specific genre of music! Music by its very definition is an expression of the arts and one should be encouraged to express himself or herself artistically, but around this time in my life the style of music which I was recording was underground "garage." It had become very popular, with many songs going straight to number one on the national charts without having been promoted in the "normal" music industry fashion. There were a few individuals, however, attending garage "raves" with the intention of causing trouble.

With an increase in violence on the garage scene, the Metropolitan police soon stopped issuing licenses to anyone wanting to hold events where this genre of music was being played. A domino effect occurred when even Parliament began to talk about the increase in gun violence at garage events; radio stations soon followed suit and refused to "play list" anything from this genre in order to dispel violence at rave scenes and discourage crime. This was devastating news as my song was just about to be added to the BBC Radio One play list, which would have earned me many thousands of pounds in airplay royalties. Virgin Records also refused to shoot a video as there would be no radio play to support the video. It felt as though everything I had worked so hard to achieve was crashing down around me.

Not being one to allow obstacles to hold me back, I soon set up my own independent record label to release my own material. I started getting excellent reviews in the underground music magazines, and the song was number one on the underground charts. I had sale or return deals with all of the specialist music shops in Central London, was producing a lot of material, and was ready to become the British equivalent of Missy Elliot. The record shops soon started slowing down on the number of records they were willing to take from me, as Wiley was dominating the scene with his Eskimo franchise, so they were unwilling to take any other material.

I tried several other ventures after this time, but felt quite defeated by my whole experience and decided it was time to try something other than music. I've often heard it said that "persistence is the key," and indeed it is, but we must also be wise enough to know when to quit. "Timely retreat is the mark of the warrior" is an Old Norse saying. I lost my passion for music; I couldn't even listen to the radio because I had become so critical of everything

I'd hear, and resentful that I was unable to fulfill the career I'd always wished for in the music industry. I backed away and chose a new path. Since I'd lost my passion and drive for music, pursuing a career in the music industry would have been a waste of my energy. This is not to say I let go of the artist, but the artist took a break from the life she'd known.

SELF-EMPLOYMENT

I tenaciously sought new opportunities. I was in a good position financially, having received a large advance from Virgin, and was in receipt of royalties from my hit song. I felt hopeful that something good would soon come my way. I knew that I wanted to be self-employed, and mulled over what sort of business I would start. I'd been close to going into business with several other people, and realising that I couldn't find a good match, I decided that the only way forward was to go it alone. Still not feeling confident enough to start my own business, I looked for franchise opportunities. Within two months, I'd bought and was running my own domestic cleaning franchise which is a somewhat different lifestyle to the rave scene.

I understand now that throughout this period I always maintained my artistic ability to adapt and move forward with change. I had always been a rapper, but I used my writing ability to write songs, and adapted my rapping ability to garage and became an MC. I suppose this could also be attributed to the constant changes I had to adapt to growing up. Looking back and, "connecting the dots," I realise that these events have given me the innate ability to adjust to any situation.

There are some types of people who are not as capable of adjusting to major life changes. Many homeless people were once great scholars and businesspeople who could not see past the disappointment of losing a career or other traumatic life event changing their course.

BUSINESS SENSE

As mentioned in chapter one when describing how psychometrics works, I shared with you that I am a high "I." I am also a low "S." This is someone with a low boredom threshold, who loves variety and likes to do things at a quick pace. I even have to slow myself down as I'm speaking, as I can't wait to get my many ideas out in the open, even to the point of finishing other people's sentences. But I am aware and totally grateful from where all of this has come. Having a high "I" has given me the gift of being totally comfortable walking into a room full of strangers and striking up an instant rapport with whomever I speak. I could complain that I changed schools many times to the point of feeling like a misfit as a child, or I could celebrate, as I do, my ability to be comfortable in a room full of strangers because this is what my emotional intelligence now allows me to do. This has been a conscious choice to see a seemingly negative situation in a positive light, but this understanding that I can change my perception of who I am has only come about by knowing myself. I can understand who I am because of what I've learned through psychometrics.

Making money is something that has always motivated me (another high "I" trait), and has brought me great satisfaction in the business ventures I operated as a child as well as the businesses I run today. But more than anything else, I have always maintained a desire to succeed. D. Forbes Ley, in the excellent business book The Best Seller, says "to visualise is to desire." We don't always have the desire to do the tasks necessary to achieve success, but if one can visualise the desire, then one can certainly learn to motivate one self to have the desire. Focus on the outcome. The desire to succeed is there, and if we focus on the outcome and recognise that there are steps to take in the process, then desire for the less desirable tasks is created – all with the power of the mind!

I always saw myself being a self-employed businesswoman, and maintained the desire to fulfill that vision. When Joe Adams, my mentor, first asked me to complete the Sales Aptitude Indicator (SAI), which I refer to in chapter one, he told me that I scored eight out of a possible ten for my desire to succeed. It was later revealed to me that at Encyclopedia Britannica, where this tool was first developed and where Joe Adams was Managing Director for over thirty years, he would not employ any salesperson whose desire on the SAI was below average. Joe explained to me that "you can teach a person sales aptitude, but you cannot teach them to have desire." Desire is something that comes from within; it is personal. I say, you may not be able to teach someone to have desire, but we can show them how to motivate themselves to develop the want to have the desire via visualisation.

In Ask and It Is Given by Esther and Jerry Hicks, Abraham speaks of "launching rockets of desire," and describes this process as being instigated by contrast. The contrast is between what we have and what we want, which is what creates a desire for something new – change. Here, one can be creative in the contrasts they choose to identify. You can launch a new rocket of desire by creating contrast between a seemingly fantastic situation to a greater imagined one in order to bring about changes that will positively impact lives other than your own.

UNDERSTANDING CULTURAL AND SOCIAL INFLUENCES

B eing the daughter and granddaughter of Jamaican immigrants, I have always had somewhat of an "immigrant mindset," meaning that I have always reflected on how my life may have been had my family not left Jamaica. I have heard many stories of the poverty of their lives "back home," and have always internalised these feelings as a way of identifying the contrast between what they had to what I have now living in England, appreciating my position whilst still pushing myself forward.

When my two eldest sons, who were born nineteen months apart, were babies, I used to receive benefits from the government. I would always feel disgusted by the position I was in, and knew that if I was in Jamaica there would be no such support. This drove me to desire independence, and to want one day to be a contributor to society and give back to the benefit system which once helped me. I held that vision, and I am now in that position. It feels great paying taxes. I know that I will always earn substantially more than will affect me after tax, so I am happy with the contribution I make to society.

My focus regarding society now is more global than local, but the contrasts I have experienced in my own life have held my focus to always desire to do more for others. Albert Einstein said, "Only a life lived for others is a life worthwhile." When I was young, I would enter situations asking, "What's in it for me?" I now ask, "What can I bring to the table?"

OTHER IMMIGRANT ENTREPRENEURS

Immigrant entrepreneurs have had a monumental effect on Western business ideas and new product development. One such hugely successful immigrant to the United States is the founder and CEO of Netgear, a company largely responsible for the availability of high-speed internet connections (broadband and Ethernet) which are now standard on new computers. He helped to make the worldwide web accessible to all, but his life was no picnic. Forbes Magazine says,

"Netgear founder and CEO Patrick Lo was just nine years old when he relocated to Macao with his grandparents in 1965. He left Mao Zedong's China without his parents, who had been condemned to nearly 10 years in labour camps in the mountainous province of Canton.

Lo and his grandparents later moved to Hong Kong, where he went to high school with the dream of one day studying in the U.S. 'From a very young age, I wanted to be an electrical engineer,' says Lo. 'I'd always dreamed of coming to the U.S. for college."

And so Lo, whose family had no money, hit the books and ended up winning a full scholarship to Brown University in 1976. 'Being a very poor boy, there was no hope to pay my own way,' he says. Getting the scholarship to Brown 'was like winning the jackpot.'

After raising $400 in a fundraiser back in Hong Kong for his plane ticket, Lo was on his way to Providence, RI, to study electrical engineering. In a big hurry to start working, Lo fast-tracked his studies and graduated in three years instead of four.

A similar study from Duke University showed immigrants were responsible for starting 25.3% of all new, high-technology businesses in the U.S. during the past 10 years.

But Lo didn't set off by himself right away, working for Hewlett-Packard as an engineer back in Hong Kong for the next 10 years. 'Being typically Chinese and having been brought up in a poor family, the first thing I thought about was how to make a living,' he says. 'The easiest way to do that was to join a big company as an engineer.'

By 1995, Lo had done so well at Hewlett-Packard that he was tapped to lead HP's efforts to develop a Unix servers business in Japan that would rival those of IBM and Sun Microsystems. He cultivated a regional customer base, recruited Asian supply-chain partners to service the Japanese market and, in his spare time, managed to learn Japanese in six months by taking two-hour lessons every morning before work. Within three and a half years in Tokyo, Lo took HP's servers business from nothing to over $200 million.

Lo was knee-deep in the tech boom of the late 1990s when he approached his bosses at HP about starting a new division to target the Internet. But, he says, 'they thought [the Internet] was just a fad and it would go away pretty fast. I disagreed, so I quit.'

Not an easy decision, but one that paid off for Lo. He found a friend in his former boss, Dominic Orr, then-senior vice president of product development at Bay Networks, which at the time was as big as giants like Cisco Systems, Cabletron and 3Com. Orr liked Lo's idea of developing cheap, fast consumer hardware for connecting to the Internet and, in 1996, agreed to help fund Netgear as a subsidiary of Bay Networks.

'The first year was just atrocious, and the second year was no better,' says Lo, who liked running his own show after picking up some business tips from his time in Tokyo. 'I wasn't worried about the business because I knew we were on the right path.'

Lo still wasn't worried when, in Netgear's third year, Nortel Networks bought beleaguered Bay Networks, leaving Netgear by the wayside in 1998. From a contact at Nortel, he managed to develop a relationship at Pequot Capital, one of the biggest hedge funds in the world at the time, and secured some much-needed venture capital.

In 2006, Netgear celebrated its tenth anniversary. Walk into a Best Buy or Staples and you'll see any one of 100 different Netgear Ethernet, networking, broadband and wireless networking devices that help consumers and small businesses go online. Since 1999, the company has grown at a compound annual rate of 26%, with fiscal 2006 third-quarter revenues of $151.6 million.

Netgear is just one of the thousands of publicly traded, immigrant-founded venture-backed companies in the U.S. that together are worth more than $500 billion, according to a November study commissioned by the National Venture Capital Association. The association's research found that immigrants like Patrick Lo – who make up only 11.7% of the U.S. population – have started one in four of all U.S. public companies that have been venture-backed over the past 15 years, including Intel , Google, Yahoo! Sun and eBay.

A similar study from Duke University showed immigrants were responsible for starting 25.3% of all new, high-technology businesses in the U.S. during the past 10 years. The greatest percentage of these entrepreneurs hailed from India (26%), followed by immigrants from the U.K., China and Taiwan.

As for Lo, who now lives with his family in Silicon Valley, China represents more of a business opportunity than a home.

'Coming from China, from a poor family, I had nothing to lose, and I knew I had to work hard. That's what an entrepreneur needs,' Lo says of his entrepreneurial experiences in the U.S. 'You can't worry about losing anything, and you have to work extra hard.'

What an inspiring story. Lo's life includes obstacles which most of us reading this book do not face. We don't face the difficulties of dealing with a communist government who demands the loyalty and structured thinking as the government under which he grew up and thrived. Though many of us will reject the idea of communism as an ideal society, even such rigid structures don't limit the creativity of those who have the desire to succeed. Perhaps they have a better understanding of how giving can bring abundance back to an individual.

Sports fans will certainly recognize another US Immigrant great who recently contracted with the Los Angeles Galaxy Major League Soccer Organization. His arrival in the United States was one of the most widely publicised publicity moves in the history of sports. David Beckham signed a multi-million dollar deal with the Los Angeles team and MLS to play for the California team (while remaining a member of the official team of England) and most importantly, to invigorate soccer in the United States. Beckham did not make the move with his wife Victoria, a.k.a. Posh Spice of the hugely famous 1990s pop group "The Spice Girls," just to be part of a winning team. There is a much larger focus for this move for the British soccer star. The arrival of Beckham in the U.S. is intended to bring a greater awareness for the game of soccer to the American public. Though soccer is played and enjoyed in the U.S., there is not the focus on it as a national team sport as there is in Europe and elsewhere.

Though David and Victoria Beckham are now household names in the United Kingdom and the U.S., Beckham hails from a rather humble background. His parents were working class: his mother worked as a hairdresser and his father as a kitchen fitter. By no means was he born privileged or rich, yet, interestingly enough, is the focus David grew up with. His father was a Manchester United fan, and the child was raised with national pride and soccer as a team sport from a young age.

Though the Beckham's significant wealth is not limited to the incomes of either partner individually, their original art is what led them to the amounts of abundance they now enjoy. Sports reports in the U.S. stated that Beckham earned $200 million for his participation in the venture that took him to Los Angeles before he even stepped off the plane as an immigrant in the United States. Both he and his wife are artists who have explored and pursued outside areas such as clothing lines, photo shoots, etc. to display their art, talent and beauty.

On a side note, Beckham's first game with the Los Angeles Galaxy was not a win for Los Angeles. The D.C. United emerged victorious. With the winning attitude and "team" focus of this incredibly talented man, do you think he sees this as a setback or part of the fun of the journey on which he has embarked?

In the words of Martin Luther King, Jr., "Everybody can be great... because anybody can serve. You don't have to have a college degree to serve. You don't have to make your subject and verb agree to serve. You only need a heart full of grace, a soul generated by love." This rings true for all successful immigrants everywhere. They each had or have their niche – their contribution to society and the world.

Confucius, the ancient Chinese philosopher said, "He who wishes to secure the good of others has already secured his own." There is so much more satisfaction in giving than receiving, though to be a truly good giver, one must first understand what it is to receive. We display great acts of kindness when we understand the pleasure of the one who is receiving our gift, assistance, or compliment. Studies were done giving people the task of doing five random acts of kindness per day. At the conclusion of the study, the results showed that the giver, who may have simply held a door for someone or even simply smiled in their direction, felt happier overall than days in which they did not consciously display these actions. Giving and receiving are two sides to the same coin.

We've come to a stage in our evolution where we cannot serve ourselves without first serving others. Take, for example, Bill Gates. He is and has been the richest man in the world as ranked by Forbes Magazine since 1995. Why is he in this position? Because his products and services serve people everywhere to accomplish their tasks more efficiently everyday. Gates focused not only on creating fabulous computer software and technology which would bring him great riches, but he focused on making his products invaluable to all people. He saw a legitimate need for his services, and strove to be the best and create the best he could. His focus - to provide the best products he could and at a fair market value - made him the richest man in the world. Gates is also a philanthropist who gives back huge amounts of money to people and programmes he feels are worthwhile. He contributes money for scholarships for minorities such as the United Negro College fund, for AIDS research to help prevent and alleviate disease in third world countries, and other organisations. He continues to give back to the people who have helped make him so wealthy and so powerful.

"It is one of the most beautiful compensations of life that no man can sincerely try to help another without helping himself."

Ralph Waldo Emerson

We must recognise contrasts in our life, and always have the intention to serve in every way possible in order to fulfill those "rockets of desire" we have launched. We must adopt an "I owe you" outlook on life, as described in Smarter Selling by David Lambert and Keith Dugdale. Oftentimes, people who are born into underprivileged families develop an attitude that the world, society, or the government owes them something because they have suffered. While I do not intend to minimalise the suffering felt by anyone, it does not serve us to live with a mentality that we are owed something for nothing. We must do our part to be productive in the society in which we live, which in turn marks our effect on the world. We cannot get without giving, though we do not give to get. It is beautiful, and actually quite simple. When we give from our hearts, we get so much back. Christian scripture says it will come back "sevenfold." I say, don't worry about how many times it comes back. You may be limiting your blessings, be them financial or otherwise, by being concerned about "what's in it for me." Give, trust, and then receive.

Whilst on holiday in Jamaica many years ago, a wise woman told me, "It's not who you give to, who will give back to you." I take from that that we should give willingly with no ulterior motives, and, when we least expect it, great things will come our way. That's a universal law just like the Law of Gravity or the Law of Attraction.

So be that great person you have always dreamt you could, and indeed you should be. Cut all ties from anything or anyone who is holding you back from your success, which is your birthright. There are unfortunate circumstances in business arrangements where people feel they must claw their way to the top. Some who wish for success think that there is only a finite amount of success and business overall to be had. Some will step on others or treat others with disrespect in order to get them out of the way of their own success. They may not do this deliberately, but because of their own limiting beliefs cannot see any hope for themselves or anyone close to them without a "fight."

> I am a little pencil in the hand of a writing God who is sending a love letter to the world.

There are probably people around you who seem to wish to drag you down from what might be perceived as "too lofty goals." They see great things as happening to other people, not people from "around here." Mother Teresa said, "I am a little pencil in the hand of a writing God who is sending a love letter to the world." Most of us see the Creator as an infinite source. We don't limit God's abilities, no matter what you call Him. He is capable of all things.

We wouldn't say God couldn't give us the wealth that Bill Gates has. Yet God gave us the ability to create our own lives from the natural laws He set in motion. He gave YOU the pencil. You are writing the script of your life as you go along and you are adding a new chapter as each day passes.

Create a fascinating story, one that will inspire others to do great things for many years to come. Make it interesting and full of adventure. Do one new thing that makes you feel good everyday and start living "outside of the box." It doesn't matter how small or trivial these new thoughts and ideas may seem to be, but train your mind to always have new questions and to actively seek new answers. Do first and think later. What's the best that can happen? Turn every old belief on its head and look at life in a new way. Who wants to watch the depressing lives of people on soap operas? We get drawn into these stories because they seem to be exciting. Rarely are soap opera characters anything to write home about. Their personal lives are full of drama, deceit and chaos. These are not real lives. They're meant to dramatise relationships, but rarely do we find one worth emulating. Soap opera characters, even the ones who portray moguls, are deceptive and often get shot. The drama of these shows keep us sucked in and powerless, looking at how only the unscrupulous people get love and money.

That just isn't true. Get out into the world and build real relationships, enjoy new friendships, and have a conversation about something new. Just do one small thing everyday, whether it is adding a new ingredient to your dinner, walking instead of driving, or reading more books like this. Embrace life and enjoy every step of your journey. Find the passion in your life and live for a greater cause. The late, great Rev. Dr. Martin Luther King, Jr. also said, *"An individual has not started living until he can rise above the narrow confines of his individualistic concerns to the broader concerns of all humanity."*

YOUR DIMENSION OF GREATNESS

No one can know the potential,

Of a life that is committed to win;

With courage – the challenge it faces,

To achieve great success in the end!

So, explore the Dimension of Greatness,

And believe that the world CAN be won;

By a mind that is fully committed,

KNOWING the task can be done!

Your world has no place for the skeptic,

No room for the DOUBTER to stand;

To weaken your firm resolution

That you CAN EXCEL in this land!

We must have VISION TO SEE our potential,

And FAITH TO BELIEVE that we can;

Then COURAGE TO ACT with conviction,

To become what GOD MEANT us to be!

So, possess the strength and the courage,

To conquer WHATEVER you choose;

It's the person WHO NEVER GETS STARTED,

That is destined FOREVER to lose!

Anonymous

"Obedience is the mother of success, and success the parent of salvation."

Aeschylus

Unintended Outcomes -
Responding With Focus
Rather than Reacting With Emotions

Chapter Six

Unintended Outcomes - Responding With Focus Rather Than Reacting With Emotions

No human has lived a life without obstacles or plans gone awry. Part of the beauty of life is in the challenges we face. Somehow many people get a notion that one minor disruption to the day is grounds for giving up hope for enjoying it and, perhaps, the gorgeous sunset is missed at the end. Let's take, for example, a situation many of us face from time to time. We have a whole day toward which we may be looking with eager anticipation. We know we must wake up early. Then the alarm fails to go off. It can totally disrupt a schedule if we oversleep, that is true, but how we allow this one bump in the road to affect us or what we do with the rest of the day is totally within our control. All we have to do is start the day with a smile, and then adjust to the schedule. Perhaps we have a meal on the move. Perhaps we reprioritise the entire day.

This is what I mean by responding with focus rather than reacting with negative emotions. Often people let the emotions mount, build and continue to build so that a day starting off with oversleeping then leads to a frustrated time in traffic or nuisances as we commute to the office, short fuses with co-workers, sniggering behind the bosses back, gossip, spilled tea, and, of course, a photocopier that won't work because it is a beast whose mission it is to frustrate already annoyed workers. It is so much simpler and effective to smile, let it go, and decide to still have a nice day no matter what the agenda of the day is.

The examples of how to put this in practice are numerous. If we first put into practice smiling at an obstacle, then we can usually figure out the best way to maneuver around or over it. We can overcome obstacles with our focus – our intention. It takes a lot of practice, however, to teach oneself to respond versus react.

MY OWN PATH

E ven when my path was seemingly smooth, there were many outcomes which I could not have predicted or ever expected. I have experienced obstacle-free journeys which have ended in what I saw at the time to be a catastrophe. Only hindsight can bring clarity to a situation, and indeed, the realisation that many situations which seem hard to bear at the time really are for the best in the long run.

Imagine if I had gained the exposure I would have loved as an artist. I may never have gone on to achieve many of my accomplishments since, or I may not even have written this book! Or maybe my RAS did not allow

My point here is that we often need to be aware of opportunities that are knocking all around us.

me to focus solely on opportunities within the music industry, since I knew deep down that there was a greater calling for me where I could reach more people. Many of my friends who continued in the music industry after I left it have still not fulfilled many of their goals. Many have been signed and dropped, whilst others are living in hope of one day being discovered by a major record label and signed up in a massive deal. My point here is that we often need to be aware of opportunities that are knocking all around us. When we take the time to become aware of the obstacles in our path, examine the redirection it forces us into, and then go in a new direction with the same focus, it often opens doors of unfathomable opportunity. Yes, one might have limited oneself, like my friends waiting on that large record label signing, versus producing something else. There is an old adage, "It is easier to guide a rolling boulder." If we are moving and working with our goals and plans, we can more easily adjust to challenges than if we're only set on one possible outcome.

THE JOY OF MOTHERHOOD

If I had been in a continuous relationship all along, I may have never understood the plight of single mothers, a predicament which I used to frown upon. Obviously I can never know what the outcome of any other choice in this area of my life other than the one I took would have led to, but we must always know, not just believe, that this is the right thing for us to do at this time. I cannot imagine life without my three beautiful boys, and I am grateful for the challenges they bring to me daily (though sometimes I may need to remind myself that I'm grateful for the trips to the accident and emergency room, etc.) So many things take place in our lives in order for us to grow and develop emotional intelligence. As I stated in chapter five, giving as a mother is far greater than receiving. I'd say most mothers want to receive their children's smiles, laughter and "aha!" moments more than anything else.

Many times we disregard the lessons in "failures," and become embittered and frustrated. As I explained in the previous chapter, my feelings of defeat when being unable to further my music career could have led me to feelings of worthlessness, which may have led to a change in my self-image. Our self-image, along with our psychometric profile, can be impacted by the circumstances we experience. I admit, for a time I did doubt if I could get past the obstacles I faced and questioned if I had the passion and drive for anything other than music. What I did, and what I recommend one does when faced with such a dilemma, is to think about what it is about that job, profession, or role that gives you such satisfaction. What drives you to want to do it? When I made an evaluation of my motivating factors at the time I decided to leave the music industry, I realised that people were important to me. I would bare a lot of myself in my lyrics, as many artists do, in the attempt to inspire others to feel better about their lives, whatever their situation. This switched on a 100-watt light bulb in my head, which had been a mere flicker up until then. I realised that I wanted to touch people, and that I was here to serve. When you realise what your purpose is, it doesn't matter if your goals change because now you know exactly what needs to be applied in order to fulfill any goal. You have a purpose.

When at a similar crossroads, some people may become doubtful of themselves as I did for a while. Others may begin to procrastinate as a way of avoiding further pain or disappointment. But just because these are common things to do does not make it good to do them. Often, homeless individuals are those who were once highly educated and successful individuals who could not cope with the disappointment and change that came their way, whether or not they accept that they attracted it anyway. How sad to give up on life because one can't find the solution to a bump in the road or a destroyed career.

As I said before, the most important things in life to me are people. If I have my wonderful family, with all of their flaws and idiosyncrasies (and all families have them no matter what their place in society or financial status), then I can face and overcome any and all challenges. I think it is my duty as a mother, public speaker and author to share this wonderful attitude of competent self-image with my children and whomever else would like more information on it. When seeds of doubt creep in on our thought processes and remain there for an extended period, we must take action to replace them with positive thoughts of our abilities in order to get ourselves moving in a better direction. Pity parties are really no fun, so if you throw one and no one comes, that's good enough reason not to throw another.

Aristotle said, "We are what we repeatedly do; excellence then, is not an act, but a habit." We need to get on with what needs to be done, and to maintain a positive self-image until it becomes habitual. We must take small steps daily that take us in the direction of our aspirations. We must replace our bad or negative habits with good and positive ones, and this does take practice. If we "buy into" any doubts, we may allow ourselves to feel the negative emotions associated with these doubts and insecurities, and then our actions can never be ones to lead us to successful results.

HOW WE RELATE TO OTHERS

This approach is also successful in how we choose to relate to others as well as circumstances. We can think about the outcome to a certain statement, a look, or a non-response. **Words form only 7% or so of our communication**, and the rest is 38% tonality and 55% body language. When we act in a dismissive manner, we know what we are doing and why we are doing it, even if we are not consciously aware that we are. Yet if the result we were expecting backfires, we may deny our intentions and try to persuade the other party that we meant no harm.

Long-sightedness, or vision, must be developed in all we do. This does not need to be done to the point of planning every move as though it's a game of chess. One must think toward the eventual outcomes in order to maintain harmony in our relationships. I've heard it asked regarding relationships, "Do you want to be right, or do you want to be happy?" In many situations, we can be both right and happy once we change our perception of what right is. Ideally, we aim to create win-win situations for complete harmony. When you understand that another person's motivating factors can be very different from your own, you realise that each person seeks a different payoff in any given scenario. Tony Robbins often speaks of the Six Human Needs. The Four Fundamental Needs are certainty, uncertainty (variety), significance, and connection. He then further explains that the other two elements or needs - fulfillment and happiness - cannot be attained without the inclusion of growth and contribution. So if one person seeks significance whilst another is happy with connection, both will feel they are right in what they intend to achieve and will be fulfilled in doing so, though we will always be seeking to satisfy all six needs in whatever we do. A key to getting along with other human beings is to first realise that not everyone seeks the same payoff. And it is good that we don't. It makes the world a much more interesting place. Diversity is finally being valued worldwide. How happy do you think our friend Olaudah Equiano, the former slave who bought his freedom mentioned in chapter one, would be with this evolution in thought?

ACTIONS FOR POSITIVE OUTCOMES

In The Rules of Life by Richard Templar, rule number 13 is, "No Fear, No Surprise, No Hesitation, No Doubt." He took this from a 17th-century Samurai warrior who used these as his four-point key to successful living and swordsmanship. As with most philosophies and philosophical theories and practices, this can be adapted to other circumstances. I would like to further elaborate on this in the context of being prepared for unintended outcomes.

FEAR

Love and fear are the headlining emotions we are able to express. All the other emotions are just subcategories of these. We are in a constant motion of moving away from fear and toward love. In our fearful expressions of jealousy, and even hate, we cannot feel love. The only way to eliminate negative emotions is to eliminate fear.

SURPRISE

If we expect the unexpected, then there should be little to surprise us. Not that we'd wish to expect doom and gloom, but we'd be prepared enough to have a contingency plan to soften the blow. Isaac Asimov wrote, "The only constant is change, continuing change, inevitable change that is the dominant factor in society today. No sensible decision can be made any longer without taking into account not only the world as it is, but the world as it will be." Life is full of unexpected experiences. If we are prepared to just expect the unexpected, then we can look at these redirections with eager anticipation, or at least less dread, and not have them throw us off course and ruin not only our day, but the path or journey on which we focus. They can be the downshifting we need in order to really enjoy what is around us at the moment, thereby creating more of what we want than we initially imagined!

HESITATION

I feel that hesitation is closely tied with doubt. We hesitate when we are uncertain, and that uncertainty is what ultimately leads us to failure. Others will detect that we are "being backward in coming forward," and may become suspicious of our intentions. Hesitation is also part of the procrastination family, which is simply to defer an action. Hesitation is not the same thing as slowing down. If you consider what occurs when a car "hesitates," it is the literal momentary stalling of going forward or a brief "stop." Surprises, as mentioned above, may have a hesitating effect on us, but with practice we can keep ourselves on the path and redirect versus needing to come to a stop to figure out where to go next. The key to this is in releasing the fear that causes us to hesitate.

DOUBT

Doubt brings us full circle back to fear. Confidence erases all doubt. Be open to making mistakes but never doubt your ability to get over them. Be confident that your actions will take you in the direction in which you will learn most, and know that only application can reveal your strengths and bring you more confidence. Continuing with the automobile analogy, if one was driving and came into some traffic, it should not deter us from the journey to the intended destination. We find other routes which, in the case of stopped traffic, will keep us moving on what otherwise may have been a slower route.

But because of the "surprise" in one's path, the other route, which still arrives at the same destination, is the more appropriate choice. I find that the back country roads of small towns and cities are often much more beautiful and educational than the rapid, sterile route of the motorway, autobahn or other path meant to simply get one from point A to point B in the quickest time.

CRYSTALLISING YOUR GOALS

What do you have the single most desire to do? What keeps you awake at night or gets you out of bed in the morning? Take money out of the equation for a while, and let's imagine we live in a money-free society where you have everything you please at your disposal. How would you spend your days? What would bring fulfillment to your life? What would you be most happy doing?

I heard a story recently of an osteopath who wants to give up his job to become a postman. Maybe it's not being a postman that appeals to him as much as being outdoors, providing a reliable service to the public, and staying fit whilst doing so. Osteopathy is a very well-paid profession, and he happens to run a private practice with his father but cannot see himself (to see is to visualize, which in turn creates a desire) doing that for the rest of his life in the same way his father did. If we are to truly enjoy life - enjoying each day, slowing down to take the back roads, spending time outdoors - then isn't the postman position a better choice of career for that osteopath? It may be an extreme example; however, if you reprioritise your life, taking the issue of money out just for the time being, then finding out what is truly important to you is imperative for determining how you want to spend your time earning or creating income.

In crystallising our goals, the whys are always more important than the hows. The hows will only lead you into further confusion, whereas the whys will drive you emotionally, convincing your subconscious mind to believe that the thought held is true and will dictate new actions for the desired result. Since becoming a mother, I have been driven to give my sons as many options as possible for the future. One of my closest cousins is serving a 25-year prison sentence, whilst at least four other family members are battling with crack, heroin, and alcohol addiction. For some reason, and perhaps because of their present situations, they have been unable to see any options other than crime, promiscuity and a "you owe me" mentality.

I am driven to show my sons that that reality does not need to become their own, and further show them all the options available to them until they start to point out other options to me which I may have missed.

A FAMILIAR DEPICTION OF VISUALISING GOALS

Most of us are familiar with the 1930s classic film, The Wizard of Oz. Many of you may have also seen the performance of young – only six years old – Connie Talbot of the song Over the Rainbow on "Britain's Got Talent." If you aren't, please seek it out on Youtube.com or elsewhere. It is truly inspirational. Even mean old Simon couldn't hold back praise for this child.

But let's look at the story of the Wizard of Oz. Our heroine, Dorothy, has one goal: She wants to get back home from a land of enchantment where she encounters so many obstacles inhibiting her on her mission. Yet in the process, she establishes friendships with three very unlikely candidates. In fact, they don't exist as possibilities in her reality. One can't often become friends with a Tin Man, Cowardly Lion or Scarecrow whilst remaining outside the confines of a mental institution. But they exist in Dorothy's mind, and come to life in her dream to help her sort out her fears and propel her on her journey to reunite with what is important to her – her family.

In the end, the intended and hoped for destination, as it is exposed to her, was all in her mind. She had to figure out the elements in her mind, appreciate the life she had and then, her dreams came true - because first she dared to dream.

OVER THE RAINBOW

Somewhere over the rainbow

Way up high

There's a land that I heard of

Once in a lullaby

Somewhere over the rainbow

Skies are blue

And the dreams that you dare to dream

Really do come true

Some day I'll wish upon a star

And wake up where the clouds are far behind me

Where troubles melt like lemondrops

Away above the chimney tops

That's where you'll find me

Arlen-Harburg

"The most successful men in the end are those whose success is the result of steady accretion. . . It is the man who carefully advances step by step, with his mind becoming wider and wider – and progressively better able to grasp any theme or situation – persevering in what he knows to be practical, and concentrating his thought upon it, who is bound to succeed in the greatest degree."

Alexander Graham Bell

Chapter Seven

Seven Levels of Self Awareness for Success

Chapter Seven

Seven Levels of Self Awareness for Success

"May you live your life as if the maxim of your actions were to become universal law."

Immanuel Kant

Okay, I know by now you may be thinking, "So why is 'we' the new 'me'?" Before I answer this question, I would first like to reveal the seven levels of self awareness for success. In his book *The Seven Spiritual Laws of Success*, Deepak Chopra describes these laws as:

1. **Pure potentiality**

2. **Giving**

3. **Cause and effect**

4. **Least effort**

5. **Intention and desire**

6. **Detachment**

7. **Purpose in life**

Each of these laws has been explained to some extent in the previous chapters, but for further clarity I would like to introduce the Seven Universal Laws which are:

THE LAW OF PERPETUAL TRANSMUTATION

E nergy is, and energy is forever changing - moving into physical form and back to pure energy again. Energy is in a constant state of transmission and transmutation.

- Everything is growing or dying, becoming permanent or passing, increasing or decreasing.

- The images you hold in your mind most often manifest into physical results.

- If you really look at the elements of the Law of Perpetual Transmutation, the ideas are probably not even foreign to you. You might apply the definition of energy to the definition of God. You might see that the second bullet point is sometimes referred to as "the circle of life." These are just different ways of expressing the same truths.

THE LAW OF RELATIVITY

- Nothing is good or bad, big or small until you RELATE it to something else.

- Everything "just is" in comparison to something else.

- There are, however, moral absolutes.

- If you relate your problems to something much worse, you will get a different perspective.

L et's expand on this idea of relativity. As humans, we need to relate things to their opposites in order to understand them. Yet, as we mature and increase in our ability to use our minds, then we are capable of abstract thinking. We have to be ready to think abstractly. The idea that nothing is really good or bad until you relate it to something else may be new, but you are capable of it as an adult because you've developed your mind. Since you've read the first six chapters of this book, you have an even greater understanding of the mind. It's all relative.

THE LAW OF VIBRATION (THE LAW OF ATTRACTION IS A SUB-LAW OF THIS LAW)

*   Everything vibrates; nothing rests.

*   There are various levels of vibration or "frequency."

*   Conscious awareness of your vibrations is your feelings.

*   The higher the density, the higher the speed of vibration. The lower the density, the lower the speed of vibration.

D epending on your upbringing and education, some may react to the Law of Vibration with a smirk or dismissal of hippie ideas, but this is a law of science, too. In fact, it is a law we get from science. Taken down to the smallest particles in the universe, everything vibrates. If you could look through an electron microscope, you'd see that that stationary boulder on the hill is indeed vibrating. Why then would we expect anything different from the human life and human mind with its wondrous capacities?

THE LAW OF POLARITY

- Everything has an opposite: Hot – Cold; Up – Down; Good – Bad; Male – Female.

- The opposite side of anything is always equal and opposite.

- There is a positive and a negative to everything, even people, so always highlight the good in others.

Eastern philosophies refer to this as yin/yang, and you may even recognise the symbol, which is pictured below. Note that the two opposites are symmetrical yet still opposite. They also complete a "whole." With their opposite elements, they form a perfect circle or sphere.

This is an easy one to comprehend because as children in primary school, 'opposites' is an exercise we are given to help develop our mind's capacity to understand words and concepts.

THE LAW OF RHYTHM

- Everything operates by rhythm.

- The tide goes in and out, night follows day, rising and setting of the sun, and good times – bad times.

- When you are experiencing bad times, know that good times must follow.

It is interesting to note that everything operates by rhythm, and so when we get "out of sync" with our nature or rhythm, we are "out of sorts" in a lot of ways. Check in with your integrity and see why the rhythm of life is off. One of the suggestions I make for being in a state of joy is to dance, which is such a simple way to identify rhythm, and get your groove on. I find it hard to not be happy when dancing. So if you know good times follow bad, then dance. The good times are on the way.

THE LAW OF CAUSE AND EFFECT

- Every cause has an effect and every effect has its cause.

- Ralph Waldo Emerson called the Law of Cause and Effect "the law of laws."

- Look at the cause of your feelings (via your thoughts) and adjust them for your desired effect to take place.

A word that has become popular in the English language is actually from Sanskrit. It is "karma." Karma, in its most accurate form, is the sum total of your actions, but Eastern philosophies will adjust this to the idea of actions from prior lifetimes. No matter what your attitude toward reincarnation, know that because of the Law of Cause and Effect, we all produce karma in this life. Our actions, or the cause, will produce an effect; our thoughts, as causes, affect our feelings and emotions. Choose good thoughts to create good karma.

THE LAW OF GENDER

- Male and female are necessary for procreation.

- Like seeds, everything has a gestation, or incubation, period.

- Your goals will manifest at the right time.

Please visit *www.thesecretrevealed.thesgrprogram.com* for more information on how to work with these natural laws.

Once we are able to really digest the Seven Laws laid out for us by Chopra, then we can easily use them as tools as I will now suggest.

SEVEN LEVELS OF AWARENESS FOR SUCCESS

ATTITUDE

This is simply a way of thinking, and knowing that your thoughts give you your results; a positive attitude must be maintained to attract all things requisite. Our self-image will determine our attitude, which is a sum total of our thoughts, feelings, and actions, along with our attitude defining our self-image. This gives us individuality. We act "as if" until it becomes a reality, always remaining adaptable in the process. Charles R. Swindoll wrote,

"The longer I live, the more I realize the impact of attitude on life. Attitude, to me is more important than facts. It is more important than the past, than education, than money, than circumstances, than failures, than success, than what other people think or say or do. It is more important than appearances, giftedness, or skill. It will make or break a company … a club … a church … a home.

The remarkable thing is that we have a choice every day regarding the attitude we will embrace for that day. We cannot change our past ... we cannot change the fact that people will act a certain way. We cannot change the inevitable. The only thing we can do is play on the string we have, and that is our attitude. I am convinced that life is 10% what happens to me, and 90% how I react to it. And so it is with you ... we are in charge of our attitudes."

VISION

Plan everything about your goal down to the very last detail. In fact, the more details the better, but don't become attached to the details. Be open to the notion that something better than you could initially imagine is possible and probable. See the unseen. Everyone has a purpose in life, a unique or special talent to share with others. When we blend this unique talent with service to others, we experience the fulfillment of our purpose, which is the ultimate goal of all goals.

FAITH

Faith is the belief in the unseen and knowing without any shadow of a doubt that your vision will be realised. Many people have no trouble believing in "matters of faith," such as heaven or the Virgin Mary giving birth to the Messiah, but it seems a little more difficult for us to apply this belief to the intangible possibilities in our own lives. Yet that is exactly what we have to do. Whatever you've found faith in easily, visit that feeling of faith and then practice that feeling with your own visions and goals.

FOCUS

Having the persistence and determination not to be discouraged from your goal is our focus. It means having the grit to hold on when all the odds are against you and when other distractions come your way. As we've seen, even the simplest distractions or inconveniences can sometimes distract us from our easy goals – like getting to work in a good mood. Practicing our focus, and then developing it to a point where we are not easily swayed is the goal for focus.

GIVING 100%

When we give 100% of ourselves in whatever we do, we erase all doubts and uncertainties that may arise. When we're giving 100%, we don't have time for doubt and uncertainty; there is no room. You get out what you put in. No matter the outcome, we leave the situation with no regrets of wishing we'd done a better job. In our willingness to give that which we seek, we keep the abundance of this universal law circulating in our lives. Every action generates a force of energy that returns to us in like kind; what we sow is what we reap, to borrow a familiar analogy from the Bible. When we cause actions that bring happiness and success to others, the effect is happiness and success.

"Good, better, best, never let it rest, til your good is better,
and your better best."

Anonymous

INTEGRITY

The word integrity comes from the Latin word integritas, meaning "wholeness." To be whole is to not leave anything out, to not have anything to hide, or to be complete. We must be honest in all our endeavours, namely honesty with ourselves, our intentions, and our motives. When we are totally honest with ourselves in all of these areas, then it is not likely that we can be dishonest with others. Referring back to the idea of wholeness, if we are wholly honest, there is no room in the completeness of our integrity for dishonesty. It's that simple.

START NOW

When we introduce an intention, we put this power to work for us. We know not when our idea will come into fruition; we only know that it will, so we must put our energy into starting things immediately. If we do one thing each day for three months, no matter how small it is, at the end of three months, which is almost 100 days, we will have fulfilled 100% of our plan.

I can't say enough about starting. It is easier to guide that rolling boulder. Procrastination and hesitation will hinder us like no other bad habits can. The universe, made up of the constant flow of energy, likes activity and movement. Lead and the universe can follow. Create thoughts that manifest into ideas, which lead to actions and outcomes.

In the fantastic book S.U.M.O. Your Relationships by Paul McGee, he gives us seven S.U.M.O. (Shut Up, Move On) questions to ask when facing challenges:

- Where is this issue on a scale of 1-10? (10 = death)

- How important will it be in the next six months?

- Is my response appropriate and effective?

- How can I influence or improve the situation?

- What can I learn from this?

- What will I do differently next time?

- What can I find that's positive in this situation?

Question one asks us to apply the Law of Relativity, which gives us a clearer perspective on our situation. It allows us to adjust our attitude according to how severe we feel the issue is.

The Law of Perpetual Transmutation helps us better to answer question two. If the situation will be unimportant in six months, it probably isn't as severe as first anticipated. Having the faith to know that everything will be okay, and that this situation is indeed about to pass, will carry us through to see the manifestation of our visions and goals.

Our integrity comes into question when we react in an inappropriate manner. So in answering question three we must first be honest with ourselves. As I said earlier, if you practice integrity with yourself, there is no room to be anything but honest with everyone and every situation you face every day. Vision must be applied when deciding how to improve a situation. We need to see the improvement taking place, no matter how negative the situation may be.

We all know that for us to grow we must learn. Albert Einstein said, "The only thing that interferes with my learning is my education." So in order to grow, we must forget (or make room in our sometimes crowded minds) that which we already know to learn something new in each situation. If we are too dogmatic in our approaches to life, we will hinder growth and creativity. Creativity is fundamentally necessary to producing results for our visions and goals.

Detachment, however, is what allows us to do things differently in the future. We must separate ourselves from any negative experiences of the past so we can move forward and do things in new, more productive ways in the future. We must be willing to see where our attachments to seeing things being done in only one fashion may be a hindrance. When we detach or release the attachments, the energy flow of the project or idea can burst forth like a river once the dam has been opened.

The Law of Polarity tells us that if something is negative, to the same degree it must be positive. Every question has an answer and every problem presents a solution. Asking the right positive questions in a negative situation will present us with positive solutions. It can be helpful to identify what we don't want. The Law of Relativity and primary school trained us that way. Now let us use this to our advantage to not dwell or create that which we do not want, but to change it to a positive view and create what we do want.

THE SEVEN LEVELS OF AWARENESS

1. Animal – react. Fight or flight.

2. Mass – follow the masses.

3. Aspiration – you desire something greater.

4. Individual – you express your uniqueness.

5. Discipline – give yourself a command and follow it.

6. Experience – you are in control of new actions; if you slip off, you know how to get back on track. Your actions change your results.

7. Mastery – respond. Think and plan.

SEVEN "I"S

To create synergy within a team, we must first concentrate on each individual within that team. This is the reason for practice drills in sporting games. Before the team shows up for a match, the team practices focusing on the individual strengths of each player and attempts to remedy the weaknesses of each player. Then the "goal" of the practice, or the rehearsal, say, of a stage production or team, is to combine the strengths of each participant to unite in a synergistic match, play or other production. It is an idea that is applied all around us. Sales teams have similar trainings and seminars. We first focus on each artist in all of these team dynamics and then create one team that works in a synergistic fashion.

INDIVIDUALS

We gain an understanding of each individual using the psychometric tools described in this book. Without knowledge of where we are, one has no hope of knowing where one is going. This contrast is what creates solutions. Recognise weaknesses or what we don't want, and use the comparison to find the solution.

INTEREST

Each individual must place their interest in the aim of the group to share one single vision. 1+1=1 in the shared vision. By first understanding the individuals in the group, self-interest can be addressed in line with the overall interest of the group. Most groups have the simple goal of "winning." But do they focus on winning just one match? No, they focus on winning each match in order to be champions. Sales teams have an ultimate goal of not only each team member's income being the best it can be, but the bottom line financial figure of the company is also the ultimate goal. When each team member of a sales group wins, the company wins. Actually, if only most of the team members produce, then the company wins. Teams can be hugely successful with weak or ineffective members, yet those members frequently face the realisation that they must adapt or rise up to meet the levels of success of the entire team or they'll find themselves in another job.

INFLUENCE

Without first understanding the self-interest of others, we cannot even attempt to go about influencing them. Our influence is only taken notice of when we understand others. Understanding of others and their influences cannot come about without trying to understand others. Take for instance what you think you know about what someone else believes in the area of spirituality. Many people let this one issue hinder their ability to connect with others with whom they may have many things in common. If one, however, chooses to get to know the individual and accept that, though they are in a different place than oneself, one may find oneself with not only a new friend but also with a new way of finding solutions because one allowed the other to open up and share other paths. This can be applied in any area of life. We have to be open to influence, take what is valuable and what we see as truth, and then be willing to examine it without judgment. You won't always be inspired but without some openness to others, one will not be open to letting the good influences come in.

INTEGRATION

This refers to the wholeness of the group, when all parts come together to act as a single body. We see this level of synergy in schools of fish, or a flock of birds – not just people. How awesome is the setup of the universe to explain its own laws.

INITIATIVE

Using one's ability to further the interest of the group without being prompted is essential in making last-minute decisions. This is what I mean by initiative. Each group member should be completely clear in the objective of each project so they have enough information to use their initiative at crucial moments. One learns to be a team (together everyone achieves more) player by continually rehearsing and practicing both with the team and individually.

INTUITION

Intuition is having the gift of knowing what to do instinctively. Picking up on the feelings of others and following hunches which prove to be right will only enhance a team's performance. Completely missing opportunities in which there is no time to think can put any team at an advantage or complete and utter disadvantage.

Intuition is not limited to just Mums, but we all know she has a "woman's intuition." It is often a source of amazement to children when she "just knew." Women seem to hone these skills of "mother's intuition" because we practice it. The same phenomenon happens in teams of all sorts, not just family teams. When we learn the dynamics of the team, anticipate the actions and reactions of the teammates, unexpected obstacles or surprises can often be met with the intuition of a team member who then has the other players follow this move where it can lead to an unimagined goal or score. The intuition of the individual, backed up by the well-rehearsed team has led to many victories in sports, business, and yes, even families.

IGNORANCE

I quoted Albert Einstein earlier in this chapter where he mentions education being an obstacle. At times, in admitting we know little, we learn the most. Ignorance is bliss when it leads us to new knowledge. Be comfortable saying "I don't know," but then see where this admission might take you when you seek the information you need. Some of the greatest professors say, "I really don't know but I'll find out." Or, they may say to the student, "I don't know. Why don't YOU look it up for us?" In the latter move, the teacher has inspired the student to seek a solution.

"I" IS NO EGO

To create a dynamic team you must see 'we' as the 'I'. You need everything from ideas to infrastructure, and the willingness to implement the "I." The "I" is by no means the "I" as in ego. This ingredient must be left out with no exceptions, to even take the first steps toward success in team building. The "I" as in ego will destroy the development of the team, and, rather than creating synergy, it will separate you from others.

With the understanding that all emotions fall under the headings of love or fear, we realise that with love we feel connectedness, whilst fear keeps us isolated. As the saying goes, "There's no 'I' in team," and this is what is meant by "I." We must think of the benefits for the team before we consider our own personal rewards. There's not much to celebrate when you're the only one laughing. Success soon wears thin when there's no camaraderie.

Teams are made up of between four and eight individuals for the purposes discussed in this book. Three people make a triumvirate, whilst two people make a partnership. When the numbers are larger than eight, the "meta" (from the Greek meaning "among") team then naturally divides into sub-teams.

So what holds a team together? In addition to carrying out psychometric profiles on each individual in the group to choose the right people to establish the most synergistic team, we will need to motivate them. In simple terms, motivation can be considered as the amount of effort an individual is willing to put into what they do. Therefore, it is important to ensure that any team is highly motivated towards their goal. A lack of motivation in any member of a team can have a negative affect, reducing the group's effectiveness and possibly leading to the stifling of other's motivation. In understanding that different people are motivated in different ways, the problem facing someone in the role of leader is to create an environment in which each individual fulfils their potential.

It is important to highlight the major influences in the motivation of people. Motivation occurs when people have job satisfaction. Job satisfaction can be improved by increasing opportunities for:

- Recognition

- Achievement

- Responsibility

- Career advancement

Many companies reward their employees with cash incentives, but having spoken to many individuals who have received appraisal in this way, I have found that they would have preferred being genuinely valued or even just listened to. Understanding individuals is what puts you in a position to know what will motivate them best. For many people, you will need to identify progress and acknowledge their achievements in order to motivate them. Every team needs a leader who will instill a high level of group morale. Then people will work harder and achieve more.

Hip-hop crews are a great example of team synergy and channeling collective energy into meeting goals effectively. Each crew member will focus their undivided attention on giving a fellow crew member the push necessary for a solo release. Initially the group will build their repertoire as a collective, then once the "buzz" is built around the crew, and the profile of each individual member is such to warrant a solo project, all efforts are then put into the whole crew focusing on each crew member's solo material. This process ensures the best quality release possible with each crew member having their turn in the spotlight. Similar efforts are put in place for merchandising and product lines, which many hip-hop crews today have as an additional stream of income.

Another excellent example of synergistic groups are indigenous groups or "tribes." A well-respected anthropologist of the early 20th century, Ruth Benedict studied Native American tribes. I think to say she was well-respected is an understatement. She was one of the first female anthropologists, and she was the teacher of renowned behaviouralist Margaret Mead. Benedict's ideas on group dynamics have changed our understanding of groups or "team dynamics."

First, let us define a tribe. Webster's Dictionary gives us the following:

Main Entry: **tribe**
Function: *noun*
Etymology: Middle English, from Latin tribus, a division of the Roman people, tribe
1a: a social group comprising numerous families, clans, or generations together with slaves, dependents, or adopted strangers b: a political division of the Roman people originally representing one of the three original **tribes** of ancient Rome c: **PHYLE**
2: a group of persons having a common character, occupation, or interest

These two - 1a and 2 - certainly fit the description of what we're discussing here. So Ruth Benedict studied these groups in the Americas and found something inexplicable. There seem to be some results that occur, some group dynamics that seemingly make no sense when one examines the individuals themselves. She is credited with introducing the idea of synergy into social science. Benedict felt intuitively that several tribes - the Zuni, the Arapesh and the Dakota - had something vital, secure and likable about them, while the Chuckchee, the Ojibwa, the Dobu and the Kwakiutl gave her the shivers. Examining all her data and all variables she knew of didn't give her any clue why. She then made an intuitive leap and stated that a pattern might emerge in a whole that didn't appear in any of the parts. She termed it "synergy." She wrote in her famous book released in 1928 based on her studies of these groups, Patterns of Culture,

"From all comparative material the conclusion emerges that societies where non-aggression is conspicuous have social orders in which the individual by the same act and at the same time serves his own advantage and that of the group ... not because people are unselfish and put social obligations above personal desires, but when social arrangements make these identical."

There are some key words in Benedict's information listed above. She mentions "…societies where non-aggression is conspicuous." In other words, these are peaceful people with a common goal. But the team dynamics make "social obligations and personal desires…identical." Successful tribes, or indigenous groups, thought of as savages and sub-human, were actually found to be more advanced in their abilities to create and work toward a common goal than warring societies. Just some food for thought as we all visualise world peace. I think we split up into sub-groups for this, but it is something to consider as we learn to understand 'we' as the new 'me'.

"The most successful men in the end are those whose success is the result of steady accretion. . . It is the man who carefully advances step by step, with his mind becoming wider and wider – and progressively better able to grasp any theme or situation – persevering in what he knows to be practical, and concentrating his thought upon it, who is bound to succeed in the greatest degree."

Alexander Graham Bell

"Destiny is not a matter of chance, it is a matter of choice; it is not a thing to be waited for, it is a thing to be achieved."

Sir Winston Churchill

"Somehow I can't believe there are many heights that can't be scaled by a man who knows the secret of making dreams come true. This special secret can be summarized in four C's. They are: curiosity, confidence, courage, and constancy, and the greatest of these is confidence."

Walt Disney

"People rarely succeed unless they have fun in what they are doing."
Dale Carnegie

Chapter Eight

Presenting Yourself -
You Never Get a Second Chance to
Make a First Impression

Chapter Eight

Presenting Yourself - You Never Get a Second Chance to Make a First Impression

There are a lot of contradictory clichés on this subject of first impressions. "Don't judge a book by its cover," for example, is one we often find ourselves saying, but don't we often choose a book because it is simply attractive to us? It may be the cover or the title, but usually something gets our attention initially. I am not suggesting that there aren't many valuable things that may not be packaged well, but we as human beings have a conscious choice about how to present ourselves to the public. Very radical styles, like very sleek or expensive cars, draw attention from onlookers as they are meant to do. Punk rockers of the 1980s went to great extremes to draw attention to their wild hairstyles, extreme make-up, and clothing that was often already intended for the rubbish bin by their original owners. This form of self-expression is ageless.

Shakespeare's character Hamlet was dressed in black attire daily, not just at his father's funeral, He was a college student exploring the meaning of life, and he didn't find that life was a happy state for him. So he showed his emotions or mood in his outward display, and Hamlet became the role model for punk rockers and Goth people everywhere for centuries. It is not a new form of expression to dress in dark fashions when one is in a dark mood or permanent state of mind. On the flip side, overtly happy people often wear really loud, bright colours!

Yet there is a positive side to outward expression. I think it is good to show individuality and a sense of style not governed by any one mindset. Being free to mix and match patterns, materials and styles opens us up to another form of artistic creativity that we do daily. When you go to your wardrobe and choose what to wear for the day, you are making a conscious – yet, sometimes unconscious choice for how the world will "see you" today. You won't discuss Einstein's Theory of Relativity or quantum physics with all you come in contact with, so society has less chance to know what's in your mind except for the way you dress. So if you aim for success, why not dress for it?

THE DRESSING HABITS OF AN URBANITE IN LONDON

Having grown up in inner-city London but moving in a lot of very different circles, I noticed that young urbanites would look at your shoes before looking at anything else. Sure enough, the compliments would fly if you had on the latest pair of Nike trainers, or there would be simply no comment whatsoever if your footwear didn't cost above a certain price. Some cultures have a fascination with ornaments worn in the ears or nose, or fabulous headpieces, but in the U.K. and the United States, there is a fascination with footwear! Maybe it is because the feet are our physical foundation on the earth. It shows the "path we're walking." In any case, most of the world's fashion conscious societies value good shoes.

In September 1984, at age 11 when starting secondary school, I had the latest pair of Diadora trainers. They were called Diadora Borg Elite – I will never forget them. These trainers made me the most popular girl in the first year. At a time when the average pair of brand-named trainers cost around £15, my Diadora Borg Elite cost a whopping £37. All of the other children had obviously seen them in sports shops and lusted after them; but I had them.

To this day, wearing an expensive pair of shoes still makes me feel as proud and successful as those Diadora Borg Elite trainers did. Nowadays my choice of footwear is more Italian designer than Italian sports wear, but I get the same sense of pride as I did back then. I realise now that it's not what you wear but your association with it and how it makes you feel. I feel the same about the Cartier watch I wear everyday. Whether I'm dressed up or not, I always wear it. I remember when I bought my first Cartier in Hatton Gardens many years ago, and whilst being excited and wanting to show it off, I was almost scared to wear it. I guess I didn't feel worthy of it at the time. I do now. Now that I know myself and my mind, I know why I wear it.

> I realise now that it's not what you wear but your association with it and how it makes you feel.

The point I'm making here is that we must wear the perfume, clothes, or even just a smile, if that's what gives us the confidence to feel successful and attract more success into our lives. Isn't attracting more success the reason you picked up this book?

The first thing that is noticed about a person is their mood, then their clothing (including footwear. Footwear first if you're an urbanite), and finally their hair. My late grandfather would always say that a woman's hair is her beauty, and angrily quoted the Bible to me when I cut my hair to about an inch short many years ago. "But if a woman has long hair, it is a glory to her: for her hair is given to her for a covering." (1 Cor. 11:15) Some would say that is an archaic mindset, but in the eyes of Grandad, it was a real statement about a woman's character if she cut her hair.

Whether we like to admit it or not, even before a person has opened their mouth we have passed judgment on them. Nowadays, unless I have a business meeting, seminar or something similar, I'm not as bothered about what I wear. I'd like to think this gives me an air of comfort about me when others see me, but it may not. I'm comfortable with it though. I feel comfortable making the judgment about when to dress up or down depending on the situation. One certainly does not want to attend a garden party in stiletto Italian heels as one may break an ankle, nor does one want to wear gorgeous Diadora Borg Elite trainers to an evening cocktail party held indoors. Good judgment in these areas is fundamental. If you're attending a carefree event where casual style and creativity is appropriate, then do it right in the casual styles you like.

STAYING IN STYLE

I get a good feeling carrying cash; credit cards don't really do it for me. If I do buy something big, it'll be on my charge card and that's it, but cash, even if I'm not spending it, makes me feel successful. I don't spend as often as I once did, but when I do, I buy quality items that will last for as long as I like them. The worst thing in one's fashion world is to love a pair of shoes that haven't lasted and then Gucci has discontinued the line. However, one cannot spend outside one's means. Yes, intend for your means to increase daily, but spend accordingly. Save enough to have that money work for you in other areas. That's why I don't use credit cards.

I love the classic look and those are always good investments. Yes, see your business clothing as investments, because then one can dig a suit out of the wardrobe five years down the line, and people will still be asking where it was bought because it looks as good as new. Classic clothing, shoes included, will easily match with other items. Though blouses, including camisoles, may transition in and out from season to season, skirts, trousers and blazers are around longer. If one makes the investment for good business suits, whether for men or ladies, the accessorizing pieces are easily exchanged and, quite frankly, the easiest to replace with a smaller price tag.

I can't emphasize how true this is for shoes. Shoe fashions may be seasonal or yearly, but classic shoes versus trendy shoes are always a good investment. I do acknowledge, however, that having trendy shoes can be a fun expression of one's personality and mood. They aren't something you have to live with for a lifetime, but they can bring you joy. If something like a pair of shoes brings you joy and you smile, you've impacted the way people see you because, as I said earlier, the first thing people notice about you is your mood.

I am often told that I'm always smiling, and whilst feeling good makes us happy, making us want to smile, the reverse is also true – if we smile we feel great. Feeling good isn't just about smiling though; it's feeling good about what we eat, drink and even how much exercise we take. Healthy people have a glow about them. Someone may have a few extra pounds but radiate health, whereas someone with a pencil thin figure may look drawn and sickly. Good health is portrayed in what is right for you. Though obesity is never good, and being underweight is often a sign of lacking nutrients, there is an ideal for you. Finding that ideal, being comfortable with you, and then being conscious about guarding and promoting your health on a daily basis is what will make you the most beautiful you.

Our health shows in our skin, teeth, hair and fingernails, so we should also make an effort to groom ourselves well. Grooming is part of using good manners, whether it makes a difference to how you feel or not; it's polite to be well-presented for others - clean fingernails, fresh breath, personal hygiene, and ladies, waxing if and when necessary.

My big thing is my eyebrows. I have mine threaded once a week, which is an ancient Indian technique for hair removal. I would feel totally unsuccessful if I went out with bushy eyebrows with regrowth, even though it wouldn't change anything. How often are we so close to someone face-to-face that they'd examine our brows? But that would just be my awareness of being poorly groomed. It matters to me how I feel because that is the outward sign I show to others about me.

DRESSING FOR AN INTERVIEW

Most entrepreneurs begin by working for someone else initially. Even the great rap mogul P. Diddy began by learning the trade under someone else. Employers all have some sort of dress expectations. They may expect you to dress in very casual contemporary styles if you are working in the fashion industry, or they may have higher expectations of business dress or even business casual. Knowing what the dress code is for a prospective employer can be challenging, and as you'll see shortly, it isn't the key to getting the job. How you appear is. Often on job search websites, there are many resources that can help you determine what the dress code is, and therefore help you dress appropriately for an interview. I found the following by simply searching "dressing for success." It would be quite humorous if it weren't painfully true about what walks into human resource offices daily. An article in USA Today spoke about candidates for jobs wearing jeans, purple sweat suits, and spike heels or sneakers. Other applicants weren't afraid to show pierced body parts and spiked hair. Still others chewed gum or showed up in rumpled clothes or with their pants falling down. One recruiter even told a candidate with his trousers down below his hips to "Pull your pants up." According to the article, the outlandish dress costs some candidates the job.

So, though I applaud self-expression, there are certain instances when it is better to tone it down! The article continues to give pragmatic advice on dressing specifically for interviews, saying,

"In the conservative business climate I worked in at the time, appearances did matter. In other environments it isn't as important. However, it does make sense to dress your best for the interview, regardless of the dress code at the organization. If you're in doubt about how to dress for an interview, it is best to err on the side of conservatism. It is much better to be overdressed than underdressed (or undressed).

According to Kim Zoller at Image Dynamics, 55% of another person's perception of you is based on how you look. Her Dressing for Success information gives some tips on how to look your best, without necessarily spending a lot of money. Here's a quick look at the basics:

WOMEN'S INTERVIEW ATTIRE

- Solid colour, conservative suit

- Coordinated blouse

- Moderate shoes

- Limited jewellery

- Neat, professional hairstyle

- Tan or light hosiery

- Sparse make-up and perfume

- Manicured nails

- Portfolio or briefcase

MEN'S INTERVIEW ATTIRE

- Solid colour, conservative suit

- White long-sleeve shirt

- Conservative tie

- Dark socks, professional shoes

- Very limited jewellery

- Neat, professional hairstyle

- Go easy on the aftershave

- Neatly trimmed nails

- Portfolio or briefcase.

As you can see, it isn't rocket science to dress for an interview, and blowing the interview is a sure way to not get the job, whether it is your CV that causes you to not be considered or that short skirt, spiked heels, grills, or pierced eyebrow. Our expert points out a fashion tip I've already given you – the "conservative" classic suit. Keep in mind, though, one can have fun accessorizing once one has already landed a career or even just the job.

TAKING CARE OF BUSINESS

There is no argument that most of us need to move around quite a bit. Your physical stamina and energy level the day of the interview should be at its best. You should take care to be well-rested, fed and in overall as good of health in mind and body as you can be. A regular physical regime is a necessary in all healthy human lives. Finding the appropriate physical exercise that you enjoy will serve at least two purposes: it will help you maintain ideal physical health, and it will bring you joy. When you're in a state of joy, you radiate health and happiness. People then want to be around you. "I'd make a good team player" is what you're communicating. My thoughts on exercise, however, are just that simple. Make sure you love to do the exercises of your choice. It should never be a chore.

People often harp on about physical exercise but miss out exercising the brain. The physical brain, not the mind this time, is a muscle, and needs just as much stimulation as any other part of your body. My grandmother, who is 89 years old, is an absolute mental phenomenon. Her way of keeping her brain stimulated is to stay current. She's amazing! She's always up-to-date on current affairs, reality television, and local gossip. She is a local celebrity, and is called "Nan" or "Mum" by everyone in the community. How blessed I am to have her as an example of how to stay young, and to have inherited those great genes, too.

There are many studies about how to stimulate the brains of babies. They usually come right back around to the basics that babies want to see bright colours and geometric designs while still in the cot. So, if we know that we need to stimulate the mind of infants and the elderly in order to make their

http://jobsearch.about.com/od/interviewsnetworking/a/dressforsuccess.htm

brains function normally, why would we think the need for mental stimulation ends once you leave the last educational establishment you attended? It is just as necessary for a 20-year-old to continue to challenge and stimulate his or her brain as it is for an infant or my 89-year-old grandmother.

In the same vein as my theories on exercise, I think mental stimulation should be something that inspires you. If you really hate Sudoku puzzles, don't waste your time figuring them out. However, if you really love to do crossword puzzles or play trivia games, these are excellent ways to stimulate your mind. Reading is a real plus, too, but one can figure that you already engage in that at least periodically, because you have already read eight and a half chapters of this book.

Current events, however, are really a good idea for the upcoming business professional or entrepreneur. Reading newspapers, listening to news reports, and visiting websites and blogs that cover current events is an easy way to stay informed. Be careful of what you read; learn to decipher the agenda of the informer. Not everything you read or hear is true, of course, and often we can be misinformed, but that still stimulates the mind to remain mentally fit.

These practices also put you in a better position to discuss anything and everything in social and business situations. A really good discussion about current events or even history can bring joy, and we know what that does. Even debates don't have to be negative experiences. When one can "argue" one's point without becoming emotionally involved, new ideas and perspectives can shine through.

Also, if you find yourself on the outside of a conversation about which you know nothing, pay attention, especially if it something which might interest you. Should a participant in the conversation ask for your opinion, a great response is, "I don't know anything about the topic but I'm very interested, so if you don't mind, I'd like to listen. I'm learning so much about this from the two of you." They'll likely pause for a question or two, and maybe even try to win you over to a "side," but these types of discussions are educational and it's free. Education doesn't simply happen in the classroom.

Travel. Enjoy the world. Enjoy the scenery. Visit some place that interests you and look into the history. There is a lot we can glean from visiting places and getting to know the people of a given area. I heard a very witty but true story when listening to Earl Nightingale's classic recording The Strangest Secret. A couple attending a cocktail party met a man from Australia. The lady says, "We know where Australia is. That's right near Chicago isn't it, honey?" gesturing to her husband who agrees. The guest from Australia asks, "Why would you think that Australia is near Chicago?" The lady then replies, "Well, our son was in Australia, and when we wrote to him we had to send our letters to the Army office in Chicago, so we knew Australia was right around there."

Entertain at least one radical new idea each day. Often these ideas come from people who you seek to meet. The old expression "when in Rome, do as the Romans" implies that when you visit a new place, seek out their customs and food. Enjoy their music. Meet them. Dare to learn a few new phrases in another language. It will greatly improve your conversational and speaking skills overall while having fun and getting to know great people.

> # Entertain at least one radical new idea each day.

BUSINESS BEHAVIOUR IN ACTION

Personal interaction is a great way to improve your professionalism. Many people are not as comfortable as I am walking into a room full of strangers. Meeting strangers can be quite confronting for some people, but if one intends a successful career in the business world, interaction with others is so important. There is something very impressive when an individual can walk into a room, introduce him or herself to a stranger, and begin conversation. There are tips to put into practice which can help one overcome the fears. First one must "just do it," as the Nike commercials say.

1. Offer a firm hand shake and say "Hello! (smile) My name is …"

2. Ask their name if they don't offer it. Repeat it! Repeat it while looking at their face. There is something that clicks in the brain and helps us to remember a name when we look them in the eyes.

3. Ask about them. "How was your journey here? Who do you know at this party? Where are you from?" If you are familiar with anything they say, ask or comment, e.g. "You're from New York? Oh, I visited there last summer. I loved it!" Avoid making negative comments about a person's home or employer. Or, "I know Jane. She is a lovely woman and excellent singer, isn't she?" Keep it real and positive.

4. Show interest. Quire often the person to whom you have introduced yourself is also nervous, so don't expect them to carry the conversation on by asking the same of you in return. It is good manners to do so, but let's not expect more from others than we're currently trying to overcome. Nervousness is especially prevalent in business socialising.

5. One does need to be careful not to come on in a manner in which one was not intending. For example, if you aren't flirting, then be sure to watch your body language. It isn't a good idea to flirt and attempt a relationship in the business realm anyway. Direct people can be misread, but friendliness need not be put aside because we fear someone will take it as a come on.

6. Respect the person's space. In some cultures, touching is very natural. In New Orleans, for example, hugging and kissing among friends is very warm and embracing, but others find this a bit too close. The New Orleans music scene, however, is a very affectionate place and it can seem as if everyone loves you. And they do, but one must not read too much into this. You should pay attention to other's body language to see what is being communicated back. If a person seems uncomfortable with you, back off. Always end conversations with a phrase, "It was nice speaking with you." Being cut off in the middle of a conversation is insulting and can ostracize some people from you if they feel you disrespected them.

Like any other changes one tries to implement in their life, being comfortable speaking to strangers in social settings and business social settings takes practice. Think about it: have you ever seen a truly successful person interact with others, even if only as you watch them on the television? They always make eye contact, shake hands, sometimes embrace (watch that one depending on the culture), and interact. Something is driving the conversation. Be the one to rev the engine. It will help to develop confidence on your path to success. Yet always remember to listen.

A SPACE OF SUCCESS

Another thing which helps me to feel successful, whilst also helping me to stay organised and focused, is a tidy house. When my sons were still very young, I would teach them how to put their toys away and keep the place tidy. We lived in a small two-bedroom flat for a long time, and keeping the flat clean and tidy was a way for me to feel successful about the situation. I would only have felt worse about being in that flat if it was untidy on top of being small. Now keeping our four-bedroom house tidy is second nature because we developed good habits early on. It's ironic; I own a cleaning company but don't use its services because I developed the habit of cleaning as I go along when my sons were babies and now they also do the same - sometimes with a little prompting, but they get round to it eventually.

If you think that this doesn't matter as much as your physical appearance, think about it this way. Your home or office space is also an outward manifestation of what is going on with you. If your mind is cluttered and you're having difficulty sorting out something – anything – you might find you have things "scattered about." That is what your thought processes might very well be described as - scattered. If you tidy up, organise, and then try to work, you'll accomplish much more. Try it with just your office space. Tidy it up and compare how effective your workday is versus before your organising trial. Like many of the other suggestions in this book, being organised takes practice and planning.

You may find you need assistance in this area. There are services and organisations that help others with organising their lives. There are new very basic philosophies of "everything has its place," and ancient ones like Feng Shui, which work with the energy flow of your home or business. Many businesses use Feng Shui interior designers. It is an art form, no matter what you feel about the flow of energy in a space.

ORGANISING YOU

I offer a service as a "life coach" and this is part of what we do. We help you sort out and prioritise your life in order to function more effectively. Sometimes that may mean "clean up your mess." I may make suggestions from organising your cupboards to organising your relationships.

ATTRACTING THE RIGHT RELATIONSHIPS FROM THE BEGINNING

Though most of my readers will have picked up this book with the intention of creating success, abundance and affluence on a professional level, the fact remains that most of us would also like to attract a partner or maybe keep the one we have. So I'd like to just make a few comments and suggestions on this topic.

I know several stories of lifetime love affairs where one of the partners will say, "I looked just awful when we met." These stories, however, usually centre on the one in awful clothing doing something they love or something that the onlooker found impressive. Perhaps the lady was moving her own furniture into a flat, and the partner found this an impressive act of independence. Maybe she was gardening and singing while doing so. Sometimes he was working on a car and was filthy, but he still radiated happiness. In any case, first impressions in relationships are very important. The way we present ourselves will attract a person who finds the outward expression impressive.

Simply dressing as a punk rocker or urbanite will attract, respectively punk rockers and urbanites. So if what you really want is something else, then you should consider your dress. It goes back to the Law of Attraction. Like attracts like.

If, ladies, you don't want a man who is a womaniser, you may consider the style of your dress that attracts him initially. The same goes for gentlemen. If you would like a woman to respect you for your professionalism yet you're always in sports gear, consider dates with a bit more formal tone. I'm not saying it is necessary to put on a tuxedo and take her to the opera, but that might be a good idea annually for her to remember who you are, if that is who you feel you really are. If you want her to enjoy your sporting events and you hers, then keep the sports gear in good care and be sure she has some as well. You don't have to match, but that can be a way to bond over a common interest. If you want her to enjoy the football matches you love, giving gifts of team sports wear might make her more willing to join you on an outing. Ladies, if you enjoy that he is a sports fan, and you'd like to encourage this, recognising that his style is casual, one might easily give a gift of a replacement jersey and one for yourself.

My point in including this section of this chapter is that our outward expression of who we think we are as expressed in dress, including hairstyles and make-up, is something that is constantly communicating something to everyone we come in contact with. If you think about times when you know someone is having a bad day, think about how it is communicated to you. Their mood is sour, their dress is often off in some way, and there may be other indicators.

All of the music moguls we've covered in this book, too, have launched their own clothing lines. They recognised the desire of their audience to identify and express their identity via clothing. Since I have experience in a number of fields, including the hip-hop music industry, franchise ownership, and now public speaking, writing, and life coaching, I'm feeling compelled to do the same. I will be launching my own line of clothing shortly after the publication of this book. If you would like to see and try my upcoming clothing line, please visit my website.

www.wethenewme.com

I will be compiling a data base of potential clients, so if the line is not in place yet, please fill out the requested information so my staff can notify you when it is available.

ALL THAT IS GOLD
DOES NOT GLITTER

All that is gold does not glitter,

Not all those who wander are lost;

The old that is strong does not wither,

Deep roots are not reached by the frost.

From the ashes a fire shall be woken,

A light from the shadows shall spring;

Renewed shall be blade that was broken,

The crownless again shall be king.

J.R.R. Tolkien

Chapter Nine

When Your Song Hits the Charts!

Chapter Nine

When Your Song Hits the Charts!

We all have dreams of making it big. Most people entertain ideas of fame and fortune at least briefly during times of their lives. Untold numbers of teenage girls sing to their hairbrushes in front of the mirror, dreaming of the day when they become a star. Recent trends in popular culture have made shows like Britain Has Talent and American Idol some of the most-watched shows on television. The audience watches a young person's struggle, and finally arrival, at stardom. It is not without its trials; one must face Simon weekly, but in the end, someone emerges victorious. Usually the top contenders have gone on to have somewhat successful careers, despite not arriving in the number one spot or emerging top victor (Victoria?). The number one contestant gets his or her days in the spotlight, but those up there near the top also share in some of the glory.

I, as a lyricist, rose to the level of the top five. I suppose this is what Andy Warhol would have referred to as my 15 minutes of fame. My name was on the credits of a single at number four in the UK national charts in January 2003. I first became aware of this when a journalist called to interview me about my single deal with Virgin Records. She said words to the effect of, "You also wrote True didn't you? It's at number three in the midweek charts."

I was convinced that she'd made a mistake. I trawled the internet looking for the midweek charts to no avail, and bought all the music press, but I couldn't find any mention of the midweek chart, so I forgot about it until the Radio One Chart Countdown the following Sunday.

I sat anxiously by the radio, and as it got to the top five hits for the week, they played my song True amongst some other songs, which were possible number ones! My heart was pounding. Had it climbed a place? Or could it even be at number one?

As the rundown commenced, I danced around the room shouting, for my sons to join me. Then it was announced at number four. I was ecstatic. I called everyone I knew. It would be easier for me to name the people I didn't call. I was hoping that my song would stay in the top five for as long as possible and maybe even climb in the charts. True did stay in the top ten for a number of weeks after that, and it felt great knowing that I was a part of its success.

After all my years of struggling to get signed to a record label and have a hit song, they both came at once – only in two separate deals. I couldn't wait for the money to come. When it did, it was like Napoleon Hill says, "You'll wonder where it's been all those lean years." I wanted to spend, spend, and spend. I did, however, have the discipline to buy property first, along with later buying my franchise.

I then felt I had earned the right to buy myself a brand-new Mercedes. When I paid for my new car at the showroom, I had to wait six weeks for it to arrive. This felt like the longest waiting period ever. By then, my RAS was on alert, so I would spot every C200 coupe within a 100-mile radius. When I did eventually collect it, I drove all day and night until early the next morning. I found everywhere to go that day.

Knowing what I know now, there are many things which I would have done differently, but I enjoyed it at the time. I don't have a single regret. Although I didn't receive massive personal attention and fame, I can remember on a few occasions there being queues of fans asking for my autograph straight after one of my performances as an MC. After a Radio Kent road show at a shopping centre, fans queued for over an hour to get my autograph. It puzzled me. Why would they want my autograph? I even asked them if they knew who I was, and why they wanted my autograph. They'd always respond that they thought I was "heavy." I wasn't ready for fame; I just enjoyed writing and the rest followed.

Now being very clear of my purpose, I see every situation I find myself in as totally rewarding. I enjoy all aspects of what I do, apart from paperwork of course, but I have learnt to understand myself through the use of psychometric evaluation and why I like doing the things I do. Psychometrics has also helped me to understand others. Whilst I would become frustrated in the past when others were not true to their word in business, or would say things and not follow through, I now understand why some people do this and have learnt not to take it personally.

I have a greater understanding of the human condition because of my studies in psychometrics and other areas of life. Some personalities do not even realise they are not keeping their word, or they think that it doesn't matter to keep one's word, or they may just not care. It isn't personal, as I said. People who fail to keep commitments are ones who don't keep their commitments to themselves. They don't intentionally see that they've inconvenienced someone. They don't think commitments matter, so why would their participation in life reflect any differently?

For a while I had a few "hangers on" who were happy to come along for the ride. The VIP champagne lifestyle wasn't something I was ready to get used to in a hurry and seeing that the people around me were only there for that reason, along with whom I could introduce them to, all became rather shallow after a while. By no means am I complaining - I met a lot of lovely people, went to all the best nightclubs across the United Kingdom, and dined at all the nicest restaurants. But something was missing for me. I was looking for something deeper.

I realise now that what I actually sought to do was connect with others, but when those with whom I was attempting to connect saw me as a "meal ticket," it defeated the intention of what I now know to be my purpose.

MC Hammer is a very good public example of an artist who rose to the top only to come crashing down when his lavish lifestyle drove him, with him at the wheel, into bankruptcy. He was $13 million in debt when he filed for bankruptcy in the U.S. Courts. Hammer went on in the 1990s to become a minister. He has obviously survived and found a greater purpose, which is evident because he also mocks himself good-naturedly now by performing in insurance commercials in the United States. His Nationwide Insurance commercials have him performing in his signature "Hammer pants" with the crotch down at his knees and his wide, ballooned-thigh areas. He dances and sings Can't Touch This in front of what appears to be a multi-million dollar mansion. Quickly the scene changes to the obvious repossession of his home, and a larger-than-life painting of him is being removed by workers, along with other high-end belongings. A "For Sale" sign hangs conspicuously in front of his home with him sitting on the ground still in costume saying, "Life comes at you fast. That's why there's Nationwide," followed by their jingle, "Nationwide is on your side."

This willingness to see the errors of the past and move forward is the mark of a profound individual. Surely Hammer has come to peace with his choices and mismanagement of his windfalls. He had several hits and one of his albums was the first rap, although pop rap, to reach the diamond level rating (ten million records sold).

Hammer's story is not original for music sensations of any genre who cannot handle the difficulties of the sudden onset of wealth and fame. Many artists experience this same sense of emptiness and dissatisfaction, but many substitute this loss of connection with drugs and promiscuity. Luckily we see that Hammer eventually chose a different path which usually has no room for the above mentioned vices. I suppose if I didn't have the self-image that I do, I may even have fallen into these disempowering lifestyles, as I saw many around me do. Don't get me wrong; I'm no saint, but I always had a cut-off point where I felt enough was enough. I was never searching for anything, as I knew it was all within me. My vanity would remind me that these acts would only age me prematurely and make me look as though I'd "been through the wars," which was something I was more concerned with than just fitting in. Oprah Winfrey said, "If you come to fame not understanding who you are, it will define who you are." There are many artists who've found that that definition of them is something about which they would have preferred not to have learnt.

155

SURROUND YOURSELF WITH THE BEST

Finding others who you can trust and who share your idea of success is an easy feat, as I now know. I just didn't know that back then. I didn't know where to look to find the people who would support me in my purpose instead of those who wanted to come along for the ride I was on without being able to contribute more on an energetic and creative level. I should have, in retrospect, developed a team. I would always gravitate towards the people who were just like me. Many of them could talk a good game and paint beautiful pictures verbally, but unlike me, they had no intention of necessarily orchestrating their ideas. Teams need a variety of players with varied skills and talents.

I got bored with all of the talking, and slowly I became more and more self-centred. You'll notice that I didn't say selfish, as this is completely different, but I became focused enough on myself - or I could even go as far as saying I stepped out of myself - to see myself as an onlooker would in order to evaluate my life as to what was happening around me.

Through psychometrics, I have developed the understanding of who will work best with me in a partnership, a triumvirate, or in a team. I'm always full of new ideas, but when friends are sharing their ideas with me, unlike before, I will now evaluate if they just like the sound of what they're saying or if they've actually handed the idea over to their subconscious mind. There are many people who just want to speak their ideas into existence rather than developing a fool-proof plan of making the idea work. They may understand what needs to be done in theory, but lack the necessary actions required for the fulfillment of the idea. Many of these same people will resent you making a success of something they spoke about but had no intention of ever fulfilling. Luckily throughout everything, I had the support of my loving family who helped me with my children, and who would remind me of how strong I am and have always been, so I could get through anything. My family's belief in me drives me to always live up to their expectations, whilst they never make me feel pressured, and I can still admit when I'm experiencing any challenges. They always remind me how proud they are of me.

I admit I was never the best rapper, but when I got signed, I could detect peoples' attitudes towards me change, as though it was my fault that they hadn't got further in their own career, or that now it was my duty to "bring them in." It was my attitude that got me signed to Virgin. I have an unwavering work ethic; I do my best no matter what. I would be the first in the studio and the last to leave. I would write lyrics on the spot and record them in one take, and that is still my attitude towards everything I do today. Only your best is good enough. It doesn't matter if you're tired, if you've had a bad day, or if you've got ten children. You chose to do what you do, so choose something else if you cannot deliver 100%. Excuses for not meeting the agreed upon expectations are really just that - excuses. Too many failures to meet commitments will leave you with a bad reputation, and you'll find it difficult to progress in your chosen field. Yet if you're just conscious of your commitments and make every effort to rise to them, people and colleagues will see that you are someone who says what they mean, and they'll want to do business with you. If you can't commit to what is being asked of you, feel comfortable to say no; it saves embarrassment in the long run. Your reputation will become one that people seek out and recommend. Then you'll have so much business, you may have

> **Then you'll have so much business, you may have to hire others or share the load with those who share your values and ethics.**

to hire others or share the load with those who share your values and ethics. This is a good point to mention that as business people, artists, etc., our word becomes so important that when we recommend others for jobs, tasks, or as service providers, it becomes a reflection on us. Should we recommend someone or something that does not live up to the recommendation we gave it, it can damage us. Woah! How embarrassing!

Be careful who and what you recommend, and surround yourself with people of integrity so that your very circle of influence is on the same level of integrity and worthiness that you hold for your own business. Ever heard the old statement, "Tell me who your friends are, and I'll tell you who you are?"

Acting with integrity, surrounding oneself with quality people who do what they say, produce and keep their commitments will then attract more of those same types of people. Those who choose to do otherwise will find they have no room to pull their stunts in such a positive atmosphere.

NOTHING TO LOSE

By no means am I claiming to be an internationally recognised icon, but I've experienced the loneliness and isolation about which so many people at the top speak. I feel that having gone through this same experience in other areas of my life is what allows me to be fearless in striving for big goals. I have nothing to lose. I have no fear of my circle of friends changing, being rejected by a partner, or being disliked by work colleagues. I embrace the new; it's the only certainty. After all, the pain was in my past, and now I'm in control of my future. These same fears are what drive lottery winners to be in a worse position after receiving the big prize payout than they were before the win. There are hundreds of stories that are similar, but one woman who won describes her experience thus in an article on the online financial periodical called Bankrate.com,

"I won the American dream but I lost it, too. It was a very hard fall. It's called rock bottom,' says [Evelyn] Adams. 'Everybody wanted my money. Everybody had their hand out. I never learned one simple word in the English language – No. I wish I had the chance to do it all over again. I'd be much smarter about it now,' says Adams, who also lost money at the slot machines in Atlantic City."

I'd like to note that Ms. Adams choice, or addiction to gambling, is just as detrimental to one's life as is the addiction to drugs or alcohol. My point here is that without the proper choices, financial guidance, support of real friends, family and colleagues, a windfall can be a problem versus a solution for the "lucky," the artistic, and even the business-minded or driven individuals. It is imperative that we have a team, a support system, and are surrounded by people of integrity and honesty. Learn to say "no." Being able to say "no" is not negative. I'm not suggesting that we are to be greedy and not be philanthropic. This is another issue altogether. Philanthropy is a conscious

http://articles.moneycentral.msn.com/SavingandDebt/SaveMoney/8lotteryWinnersWhoLostTheirMillions.aspx choice to do something for another person or organisation. We choose. Knowing that some people just want to tag along on another's coattail, we can choose to whom we refuse to "lend" or "give" money. It is one thing to relieve another's stress. It is quite another issue to continually bail someone out financially who then continues to make bad decisions.

Fear causes famous people to press the self-sabotage button, and our friends and neighbours to stay in their comfort zone. Stepping outside the comfort zone is a way one can break free of the restraints of the negative thinking of close associates. You may find you no longer have anything in common with them, and they have nothing with you. Remember leaving school? Didn't you think you would just die if you didn't maintain the friendships you thought would last forever? Many didn't. And you have gone on, haven't you?

It may be difficult to ignore the attempts to sabotage your changing lifestyle by outsiders who aren't even aware of what they're doing. They probably feel that they're preventing you from being disappointed. We must go through life willing to take risks and being willing to learn from our mistakes. That is how we grow! But rest assured, if you seek people to join you in a path of success, positive thinking, creativity and abundance, you will find them. They are out there, and they are looking for you, too.

THERE IS NO
REST FOR SUCCESS

Success is a journey not a destination a year from
now you may wish you had started today.
Every beginner is a winner. Success is not escaping problems but facing
them creatively.
There is no success without sacrifice.
Great success always calls for great sacrifice.
Even failure can become an important ingredient to success.
Failure just means that you have not yet succeeded.
I'd rather change my mind and succeed than have my own way and fail.
Success without conflict is unrealistic.
Any person can be successful on smooth seas,
but it is the victory over the storm that gains true honor.
Success doesn't come through the way you think it comes;
it comes through the way you think.
Never settle for less than success.
Success is doing something good.
When you can, where you can, while you can.
It's better to attempt to do something great and fail,
than attempt to do nothing and succeed.
Success is not necessarily reaching your goal- but reaching the maximum
possibilities in light of the opportunities that come your way.
To keep your values on target remember to live so that when you "arrive,"
you'll have pride behind you and hope ahead of you.
The success is truly the path to heaven.
Success is never ending, because success is like the process of seed planting.
Every creative contribution like a seed planted may bear fruit.
Success finally is not what you have it is not what you do;
it is who you are, and what
you want to become of yourself.

Felix Lugo

Chapter Ten

The Good Life Awaits

Chapter Ten

The Good Life Awaits

"Give a man a fish you feed him for today; teach a man to fish you feed him for life."

Chinese Proverb

Now you've heard my story. I've come very far in life, and I still have a long way to go. I have goals. Goals are to target your wants. I adjust my goals all of the time. I meet some, readjust some, reset some, and I keep reaching for new ones. I've learned a lot about myself and other human beings. Understanding other humans is mandatory during self-exploration. We can quit finding fault with others and realise that they too are on a journey, but their path may be very different from our own. Understanding how their mind works can be helpful in maintaining healthy relationships with others who think and act differently. When you know who you're dealing with, you can understand and adapt, versus becoming frustrated, argumentative, or perplexed.

You also have some great tools for examining your own mind, getting to know yourself, and tips for how to be successful in the world of business and on into the entrepreneurial world. So what now? How do you get started? I hope the previous nine chapters have equipped you with the necessary mindset to achieve your heart's desire, but to further clarify the points I have made throughout this book, I would advise you to pay close attention to the following points.

SELF-SUFFICIENCY

When each of my two teenage sons was around ten years old, I taught them how to cook. They are able to cook all of their favourite dishes from scratch using fresh ingredients. They can use a washing machine as well as iron their own clothes. These are life skills, and teaching them how to take care of themselves as well as how to use their minds has always been my main priority as a mother.

Instructing others in getting to know themselves is a top priority to me as a mother and as a professional. I do this with my own sons and in my entrepreneurial world, too. Take the time to have the psychometric analysis done. See where your strengths are and recognise where you can seek the assistance of others. Then commit to improvement. Start with one challenge and take steps to improve certain areas of your life. Organise. See where you can improve your physical image and inner self-image. We all can. Part of the beauty of life is that there is always room for improvement. How dull life would be if we finally arrived and there was no more work to do on ourselves! Be willing to ask for help. Be willing to forgive, too. Forgiving others is much easier than forgiving ourselves, but both are so necessary. The best thing about real forgiveness is that you don't have to carry around those negative thoughts and feelings any longer. Learning how your mind works can help you to identify those behaviours that caused you to regret yourself and maybe even hurt others. The wonderful thing, though, is that behaviours can be changed. Then you are liberated from bad habits and you can move forward toward a life of prosperity, health, happiness and abundance in all areas. That is what I strive to do on a one-on-one basis with my clients.

COACHING

As a life coach, my priority is exactly the same as my mothering priorities, though coaching is an ongoing process of setting new goals as your current goals are met. The mindset I will help you to develop will enable you to meet and exceed all of your goals, even those which may seem out of your reach at this very moment. Though you will have the ability after reading this book to set and reach goals, accountability is also of paramount importance. Knowing you will have to maintain the highest integrity throughout your life journey, and knowing that there are no excuses to not meet the goals which you have set, empowers you in unimaginable ways. The sense of achievement and pride one feels knowing that they have stuck to a step-by-step plan from beginning to end and accomplished what they set out to achieve is of utmost importance to the experience. I am simply the person who helps you find clarity. I'm the one who can help you set achievable goals, but they may be ones which will scare you slightly because they are bigger than anything you've ever aimed for in the past, and I hold you accountable.

Our first step before beginning any coaching programme is to carry out a psychometric profile. Please find a sample report at the back of this book.

PSYCHOMETRIC PROFILE

Psychometric profiling is an excellent tool for management and recruiting. It is, in fact, an investment - almost an insurance policy. People are hired for their experience and fired for their personal failings. We've spoken a lot about psychometrics throughout this book, and I'd like to further elaborate here what I've learnt on the subject from my teacher Raymond Walley. The word "psychometric" is a construct of two Greek words: psyche, which is the Greek word for soul or mind, and metria, which is the Greek word for measure. The Oxford English Dictionary states that the word psychometric literally means "to measure the soul or mind." (Keep in mind that the mind is not the brain.) If we can see inside someone's mind, even to a small degree, then we have the basic ingredients of a powerful method to understanding them quickly and accurately.

There are two major classifications of psychometric instruments in use today: clinical tools and occupational tools. Clinical instruments were developed and are used to examine behaviour and test people by clinical psychologists and psychiatrists. They are a scientific method used to study human behaviour in the laboratory and to identify psychological problems and pathological states. I do not use this class of instruments in what I do.

Occupational instruments have been specially developed to measure and test aspects of skill, aptitude and behavioural reaction or response of people at work. There are legions of such instruments ranging from those requiring a chartered psychologist to administer and interpret, to those that simply require a suitably trained manager.

Occupational instruments divide yet again into two further important classifications. They are normative and ipsative. Ipsative instruments, as discussed in chapter one, measure people in terms of their own perception of themselves. Therefore, they are not tests and must never be called such. Normative instruments, however, usually compare people against pre-established norms and are therefore often tests, such as in the Sales Aptitude Indicator which I mention in chapter five that is designed to find out an individual's level of desire for material success and their aptitude for selling. Here, we must remember that desire is a function of attitude (please refer to the first level of awareness in chapter seven).

SALES APTITUDE INDICTOR AND THE STRUCTURED INTERVIEW

Aptitude for sales measures the innate qualities an individual has to sell to (or manage – it's the same thing) others. This can be taught. One could start with an individual who has zero aptitude and teach them to sell effectively, provided the desire is there.

The Structured Interview methodology will help to assess a number of important elements of emotional intelligence (EQ) including self-awareness, self-responsibility, self-insight, self-development, and maturity. These are extremely important areas in identifying where the individual is at presently in order to establish an effective way to move forward, grow and develop. Again, progress requires willingness or desire. The more sincere the desire, the greater the results.

ACHIEVING GOALS IN ALL AREAS OF OUR LIVES

It's great for people to set goals, be driven to achieve their goals, and make lots of money in the process, but that should never be at the detriment of any other area of their lives. We should aim to develop holistically in all aspects of our lives. All excess is rooted in emptiness. We must strive to maintain a healthy work-life balance, giving ourselves time to recharge the batteries and enjoy our victories. This way we enhance our relationships, our friendships and our teams. Business philosopher Jim Rohn, author of over seventeen books and a public speaker, says, "We could all use a little coaching. When we're playing the game it's hard to think of everything." The most successful individuals in the world know that they do not achieve success alone. They need the team, and they even need coaches.

Coaching helps people learn through taking action, creating sustainable and effective change. Coaching is to build a person by expectation, and they'll live up to this. We have been conditioned to focus on weakness. Remember all the red crosses your teacher would put on your work if you made a mistake? Forgive her and let it go, but understand this may have affected you.

First through psychometric evaluation, then through a structured coaching programme, your strengths are the focus unless they are flaws which may sabotage your ability for success. Again, it is good to recognise that we don't pay attention to what we don't want as a basis of comparison, but we focus and place emphasis, desire, and emotion on what we DO want.

SALES TRAINING

I teach sales teams what Joe Adams taught me: selling is honesty, sincerity, and belief in your product. To be a great salesperson, you need the following six things:

•   Desire

•   Ability

•   Human Relations

•   Goal Setting

•   Belief

•   Faith

Selling is fifty percent listening and is something you do with a person not to a person. Paul Hutsey says, "Some do, some don't, next!" Forcing a product or idea onto a person who is not in the market or not ready is not effective selling. Selling is about liking yourself. It's about your self-image and the beliefs you hold. If you believe that the market is slowing down, you will approach each sales situation as such. If you believe that only what you believe is important, and however the circumstances may appear to be has no bearing on your ability to determine your own outcome, you will succeed no matter what. In my coaching, your ability to sell will be tested using the SAI, and relevant training will be given thereafter. Also, human relations are determined by your level of EQ, which can also be developed over time with the correct training.

Many industries were born in times of recession. Take the movie industry for instance. It boomed at a time when many other industries were failing. Fearing whatever you may feel the climate to be is simply False Evidence Appearing Real (F.E.A.R). The only thing which is real is that which you believe to be so.

You'll notice that in the last chapter I said that finding others who you can trust and who share your idea of success is an easy feat, and that's because it is. I train individuals to become psychometric analysts and show them how to build an effective team. Building teams can be very complex, as having people with the same personality types on a team can compound, not compliment, any similarities. There is an art to building effective teams, but this is an art I am willing to share with others. Creating successful teams is such a fun task. Please contact me to find out more about training in this area. My information is listed in the back of this book.

Don't worry or stress if you come upon areas along your journey that you decide are not for you. Effort is never wasted when we're working on self-improvement. It is good to recognise what you don't want. Focus on what you DO want. Write out goal cards or create vision boards. See yourself in certain ways down the road, and then begin to develop a plan for the future. Put your creativity out there to help open up the streams of energy that will allow your "hit song to pay off." A great mantra, or repetitive affirmation, to repeat to yourself is, "I am so happy and grateful now that money comes to me in increasing quantities through multiple sources on a continuous basis." When you finally start to believe this statement, you'll find that you have changed your relationship with money. But we do need to open up the venues through which we can receive abundance. If we are doing nothing, it is like blocking up holes through which our money could come to us. Don't sit around waiting to get signed to a record label! Pursue those signings no matter what form they may take. Compose lyrics, write poetry, paint pictures, design some new clothing items or whatever it is you think you'd like to create. Don't limit yourself to one source of income or area of creativity. You may have to adjust the analogy to fit your paths. Just get moving. Be willing to be told "no," and even be rejected or criticised. But, instead of focusing on the injury, use these rejections and criticisms as learning experiences and opportunities for growth.

Know that you can overcome any obstacle, especially if you surround yourself with people of integrity who will support you on a path to success. Begin to let go of those who hold you back, whether they be school friends or family members. I'm not suggesting you sever ties with your family, but if this is an area where negativity comes to you, stop looking to them for support. Know that some people will not let go of their negative ideas, and just don't "own" their opinions. In other words, if what they say brings you down because of its negativity and disempowerment, don't "buy into it." They may not want you to be disappointed; that's fine. Recognise that as their love for you, and find others who can and will revel in your successes. Success is an ongoing journey, and as you strive towards your goals and relinquish self-limiting behaviour of the past, those around you may never see the new you. It may be more comfortable for them to ignore your growth as a way to justify lack of ambition in themselves. Yet their perception says nothing about the new thoughts you have adopted, and the new actions you are taking to enhance your life. We're out there just waiting for you to open the door and join us. No one can force you into success, and on the flip side, no one person can take it from you. We've seen a mogul who was involved in one of the most controversial scandals possible – attempted murder. However, he has risen above the accusations, whether true or not, and has gone on to do great things, including philanthropy. We've seen MC Hammer come back from bankruptcy after living a multi-million-dollar-a-year lifestyle, and direct his energies toward ministering to others. There is a man with a purpose and a sense of humour!

I urge you to embrace the ideas I have put forward throughout this book. I have sown the seed; now see yourself applying these ideas. MAKE A DECISION to implement the ideas to enable yourself to grow to your full potential. Remember, it starts with a decision, so make that decision today. Act on one new, or even old, idea which you may have been putting off.

SIX FEARS ALL HUMANITY HAVE

We would all agree at this point that fear is the only thing which will hold us back from reaching our goals. As a conclusion to this chapter, and indeed this book, I would like to outline the six fears all humanity have. We don't all possess all six of these fears, but most people will experience one of the six at some stage in their life. Our awareness of these limiting beliefs is what allows us to conquer them.

1. Public Speaking

2. Heights

3. Physical Infirmity

4. Death

5. Decision Making

6. Financial Destitution

You'll notice that all except one of these can be overcome using one of the techniques previously outlined. We need to get past our fears in order to move forward.

Get moving. It is much easier to change direction than to get started. Find out what your passions are and pursue them. Develop whatever artistic talents you have. Taking classes is a great way to improve skills, whether they are learning to write creatively or learning to paint. You'll also meet like-minded individuals in classes. These need not be limited to an academic setting. Motivational seminars are an excellent arena to hone skills, stimulate your mind and motivate yourself. I'll be offering services as a motivational speaker, so be sure to visit my website to see my schedule of upcoming seminars or to request information on hosting one.

Let me know what your first step will be - completing a psychometric profile or creating a mastermind group with friends and colleagues. Again, my contact information is also included in the back of this book.

Most importantly, I would love to hear your success stories.

"When you're ready for success, success is ready for you."

Jack Canfield

Watch your thoughts,

for they become words.

Watch your words,

for they become actions.

Watch your actions,

for they become habits.

Watch your habits,

for they become character.

Watch your character,

for it becomes your destiny

Frank Outlaw

A GUIDE TO INTERPRETING THIS REPORT

The following description of Adam's probable behaviour at work is based upon his subconscious knowledge of himself. It is NOT a test or an all encompassing analysis of Adam. The report is designed to be comprehensive, within the limits of the capabilities of human measurement systems. You may not recognise all the behaviours described.

However, learned behaviour skills cannot be measured by Personality Survey with precision. A naturally independent person dislikes detail and has a poor sense of time. Time management training can change this without affecting his basic independence.

Individuals acquire or develop competencies that affect the way they work and relate to people. Collectively known as "emotional intelligence" (EQ), they are known to have a greater bearing on success than intelligence quotient (IQ) or training (see Goleman "Emotional Intelligence"). Self-awareness, self-regulation, motivation, empathy and social skills are essential to the success of top performers. Clues can be found in the Personality Survey, while further information can be gained using the Structured Interview & Learning Abilities questionnaires and a test of emotional stability. Effective management also requires assertiveness skills (very different from aggression or dominance). Training in EQ and assertive techniques will considerably improve both individual and team performance.

Should you substantially disagree with the report, please refer to the provider of the report or directly to Adams & Associates (the telephone number and e-mail address are on the front page of the report).

The report that follows has been produced using Personality Survey System. International copyright and all intellectual rights are reserved and owned by:
Adams & Associates (UK) Limited.

172

Glossary of Terms
*Though we try to avoid jargon there are some terms that are essential.
The following phrases may appear in the report that follows, please refer
back for the explanation.*

Emotional Intelligence (EQ)
*A term describing that combination of self-insight, self-knowledge and
interpersonal skills that determines an individual's ability to relate with
others effectively, regardless of his or her basic personality type.*

ASSERTIVENESS
*Learned behaviour that enables an individual to moderate their
aggressive or submissive tendencies in day-to-day interactions.*

SYMPATHY versus EMPATHY
*Empathy describes an ability to understand another's problem
dispassionately, to see ways perhaps to alleviate suffering but not to
share the pain.*

*Sympathy describes the trait whereby an individual relates so strongly
with another's problem that they feel the same pain and sorrow and
effectively become part of the problem.*

Stubborn "nice"
*Used in conjunction with measurements of stubbornness. The avoidance
of that which the individual does not wish to do, without actually
refusing.*

Stubborn "nasty"
*Used in conjunction with measurements of stubbornness. A blunt refusal
to do that which the individual does not wish to do.*

STRESS
*Personality Survey's ability to measure stress in an individual is a
fortuitous by-product of the methodology. It is not a definitive indicator
and so it will always be necessary to check with the individual their
perception of the level of stress they feel they may be experiencing. If
stress is deemed to be present it is advisable to evaluate their working
environment.*

ADAM'S BASIC CHARACTER

SUMMARY

Adam is a competitive, driving and forceful individual. Someone totally committed to results and very much a self-starter. He is also accurate, possesses integrity and prefers to work within parameters and rules.

He can be a fairly quick and he likes some pace and variety in his work but dislikes routine. He delights in juggling several projects simultaneously and has a need to achieve professional results.

Adam is not oriented toward people but tends to be reserved and somewhat suspicious. Analytical and drawn to facts and data he can occasionally appear cold and calculating to others.

He tends to assess all the data and information pertinent to a problem before arriving at a solution. Where risk is involved, he will have estimated it to a high degree of probability. These solutions are then implemented quite quickly.

MOTIVATIONAL FACTORS

Adam is motivated by challenge, winning and the achievement of professional results however, not just any result but the best one that can be got with the facts and data available. He strives fervently to win but not at the cost of integrity.

ADAM'S POTENTIAL STRENGTHS

A commanding and aggressive director of people, yet fairly diplomatic, he seeks to achieve good results with speed and efficiency. He is demanding and drives himself and others very hard to achieve high standards.

ADAM'S POTENTIAL WEAKNESSES

He can be aggressive and has a strong tendency to arrogance and he is not one to suffer fools gladly. Most probably an expert in his field, he can be unforgiving of those who do not match his high standards. Adam can also be uncompromising where rules are concerned and he has a tendency to become bogged down in detail.

HIS LEARNING STYLE
Adam learns fairly quickly and often in great detail but usually with some specific end in view, or the achievement of a particular goal. For him the written word is often the best method. If it is written down he can learn it therefore he will usually be an excellent student and will probably continue the learning process into old age.

HIS QUESTIONING METHOD
He will normally want to know, "What's in it for me (or the team, company or group)?" However, this is leavened by a strong desire for integrity and the 'right' answer.

HIS CAPABILITY FOR ORGANISATION AND PLANNING
He is usually a superb organiser and planner who tends also to be very practical and who has an excellent grasp of detail. Planning and organising will be analytical and objective. He can make difficult decisions about people and organisations without letting emotions get in the way.

HIS MANAGEMENT TECHNIQUE
Highly directive and commanding he prefers to tell, give orders or rule by edict based upon precedent. This is due to a preference to deal with facts rather than emotions (but not to any inability to learn interpersonal skills) combined with a demanding, forceful style and an ability for rapid thinking and attention to detail and accuracy. Adam's strength lies in problem solving.

HIS DECISION MAKING STYLE
He makes decisions easily but not necessarily quickly based on the needs of the objective but within guidelines and parameters.

ACCEPTANCE OF MANAGERIAL RESPONSIBILITY
Adam is likely simply to take managerial responsibility and wield it with discipline and intellectual rigour. Tough, blunt and sometimes pedantic he is a hard but just and impartial task master.

HIS RESPONSE TO A TECHNICAL ENVIRONMENT
He will tend to respond well to a technical environment provided that it will allow him to achieve definable and practical goals. People like him are often experts in one or more disciplines and are always prepared to learn new things.

HIS RESPONSE TO A SALES ENVIRONMENT

Adam is likely to respond very positively to sales and marketing environments. His skill with detail is of great use here, especially in technical fields or where complex ideas are called for. People such as Adam are often entrepreneurial engineers, scientists or other professionals. He is capable of being a hard and forceful closer.

CREATIVITY

Adam is creative in solving analytical problems very quickly from a basis of facts and data.

HOW ADAM RELATES TO PEOPLE

He relates poorly to other people because he lacks empathy - but he is capable of learning the effective use of interpersonal skills). Since he is usually prepared to stand or fall by his own actions, he expects everyone else to do so as well.

HIS RESPONSE TO AUTHORITY

Adam responds well to authority. Indeed, he has a distinct preference to work within a framework or rule base. Therefore, he is likely to gravitate toward corporate command. However, he has a tendency to be independent within the rules or framework, especially in the achievement of goals and objectives.

FACTORS THAT THREATEN HIS SELF ESTEEM

Adam is one of nature's winners and he will intensely dislike losing, especially losing face or being wrong. Frequently, he will be unwilling to fight a cause he considers to be lost already and so he is quite capable of dropping it and walking away.

ADAM'S TIME SCALE

Adam's sense of time is immediate so that for him, now really does mean right now. He has a need to achieve quickly, but only good results.

FACTORS WHICH MAY DEMOTIVATE ADAM

He will be demotivated if supervised by those whom he regards as inferior to him or if deprived of challenge. The imposition of rules or time scales from external authority or excessive interaction with people can also be demotivating.

ADAM'S POTENTIAL AS A CONSULTANT

Adam has the potential to be an effective and highly motivated consultant, particularly where he is operating within his own areas of specialism and expertise. His innate creativity and ability to identify issues and present innovative solutions, can be of value to the client. Conversely, he can be demanding and blunt and he is unlikely to be willing to suffer fools. Not a natural team player but he can be effective when commanding a small group whose expertise and knowledge he respects. He will not be afraid to state unpalatable or unpopular results or recommendations.

Adam is likely to be valued by the client for his technical skills and innovative ideas, but not for his diplomacy and tact. His success as a consultant will depend to a large extent on his level of emotional intelligence (EQ), assertiveness and his knowledge of the sales process. However, Adam, as has been stated earlier, can learn rapidly and effectively that which is necessary for success.

ADAM'S POTENTIAL AS A TEAM LEADER

A team leader here refers to those qualities that are necessary in welding together a disparate group of people who develop true synergy. This is not the same as managing an individual or group.

Adam's potential as a team leader is highly debatable. Not in respect of his ability to take charge - especially in a crisis - but in his ability to use empathy and emotional intelligence to generate true synergy in a team. He is by nature a tough and uncompromising commander given to demanding strict adherence to criteria.

If he is to be successful as a leader of a team and able to generate synergy among its members he will need to improve his level of natural empathy and develop his ability to use emotional intelligence effectively. This ought not to be difficult for him since he has an innate drive, and the ability, to learn whatever is necessary to be successful. Therefore, his success as a team leader will be dependent upon his recognition of the need and utility of learning and using emotional intelligence effectively to develop empathy. Assertiveness training will also be a powerful aid in developing him as a leader.

ADAM'S POTENTIAL AS A TEAM MEMBER

A team member is an individual who shares the same aims and objectives as the team and is prepared to put aside their own needs and requirements in favour of those of the group when necessary.

Adam is unlikely to be happy or effective in such environments unless he can clearly see that there will be benefits in it for him. The team and its leader must clearly understand Adam's need to take control and apply logic and objective analysis to all problems. Given that the team can utilise his strengths and that Adam can willingly subordinate his intense need to achieve elegant results to the aims of the team, then he can make a useful contribution. One benefit of this will be a potential for Adam to increase his own levels of emotional intelligence and empathy.

HOW TO MANAGE ADAM EFFECTIVELY
Adam needs to achieve and win therefore challenge him. Agree guidelines and limits with him and let him get on with the job with as little overt supervision as possible. Allow him to take command, direct operations and make decisions that will help him achieve his and your goals.

He is capable of working in a general management role or a specialist discipline and must have the opportunity for advancement and promotion. He does not need public praise but he will want to know what he stands to gain by whatever challenge you set him and will appreciate objective opinion on his performance.

Remember that this analytical man may seem distant and cold to colleagues. If you make him responsible for enforcing rules or criteria, be aware that he is likely to be uncompromising and unforgiving.

Adam can be impatient, unsympathetic, forceful, non-empathetic and will not tolerate fools or slackers. Therefore, it will be necessary to help and encourage him to listen and be more empathetic toward his colleagues and subordinates. He learns quickly but you must be prepared to answer his questions and provide relevant data.

Adam is not afraid to take responsibility and will be prepared to account for his actions and decisions in detail.

POINTS FOR FURTHER CONSIDERATION

POSSIBLE RESPONSE TO CHANGES AT WORK
Behaviours described here indicate what Adam may THINK is necessary to be successful, or survive, in his current work environment. It is not a description of how he necessarily behaves at work. It will however, give useful clues to the environment, culture or management ethos in which he works. Potential changes to behaviour identified here are ALWAYS caused by the environment, not the individual. Some statements may appear to be contradictory and so further clarification should be sought from an Analyst or Adams & Associates directly.

To succeed or survive Adam may think he should:

(N.B. If there are no points shown here then Adam perceives no changes are necessary to his behaviour and so the environment is probably congenial to him.)

PROBABLE BEHAVIOUR UNDER PRESSURE
When placed under severe pressure, Adam's normal behaviour is likely to be modified in one or more, or all, of the following ways:

STRESS MEASUREMENT
Adam currently appears to be experiencing a negligible level of non-work related stress.

DR. BOWLER'S 16 RULES OF "THE ENERGY GAME"

1. Like energy begets like energy.

2. Doing things below the line pulls you below the line.

3. There is no such thing as "hovering." One is either moving up or down the scale (vibrationally) with each thought, activity, attitude, emotion and so on.

4. Things above the line have the power to take you above the line when you've fallen below the line.

5. Things below the line do not have the power to take you above the line – no matter how unfair that seems.

6. You cannot cheat in this energy game.

7. No one else is responsible for your falling below the line; however, others do influence (sometimes greatly) our ability to stay above the line. Therefore, we must be very careful of the company we keep.

8. It's easier to stay above the line when we surround ourselves with others who spend most of their time above the line.

9. True happiness exists above the line.

10. People who spend a lot of time below the line do not necessarily want to live above the line. If they thrive on dark (upset) energy, it is necessary for them to stay there to get their energy.

11. It is not your job to get others out of darkness (or above the line). You have enough work to do keeping yourself above the line. (This does not mean that we aren't to help others, but first we must help ourselves. True service will naturally come from us when we live in a loving state above the line.)

12. A teeny-tiny bit of lightness eradicates darkness.

13. You will fall below the line. Do not panic and judge yourself, as your self-criticism only gets you more time below the line. Acknowledge where you are and do something above the line to get you back there, fast.

14. After continued practice and perseverance at staying above the line, it does get easier at staying above the line.

15. For those traveling the "Path of Enlightenment," time below the line seems inevitable. This time helps us understand the suffering and trials of others, and helps us develop needed compassion, empathy, and understanding. So, from that perspective, time at any place in the game is valuable.

16. Add your own rules as your understanding increases.

REFERENCES

In a Pit with a Lion on a Snowy Day and ID: The True You, Mark Batterson

Life's a Pitch, Stephen Bayley and Roger Mavity

Patterns of Culture, Ruth Benedict

Listening and Communicating with Energy, Dr. Ginger Bowler

The Seven Spiritual Laws of Success, Deepak Chopra

Ask and It Is Given, Esther and Jerry Hicks

Think and Grow Rich, Napoleon Hill

Writing on Both Sides of the Brain, Put Your Heart on Paper and Write it Down, Make it Happen, Dr. Henriette Anne Klauser

Smarter Selling, David Lambert and Keith Dugdale

The Best Seller, D. Forbes Ley

The Emotions of Normal People, William Moulton Marston

S.U.M.O. Your Relationships, Paul McGee

The Rules of Life, Richard Templar

The Power of Now, Eckhart Tolle

Forbes Magazine Online, *"Immigrant Entrepreneurs."*

The Secret, DVD, Bob Proctor, Mike Dooley, Lisa Nichols, et.al.

http://www.thesecretrevealed.thesgrprogram.com

Biography of Olaudah Equiano *http://www.brycchancarey.com/equiano/*

Biography of Russell Simmons *http://www.lemonadestories.com/defjam.html*

Biographies of Jay-Z, MC Hammer and P. Diddy
http://www.wikkipedia.com

The Benefits of Floating *http://www.londonfloatcentre.com*

http://jobsearch.about.com/od/interviewsnetworking/a/dressforsuccess.htm

Contact Debbii McKoy

For information on Seminars, Coaching or for a Psychometric Analysis,

Or to share your thoughts, stories and experiences...

w, www.debbiimckoy.com
e, team@debbiimckoy.com
t, 044 208 764 2291